(1) Signs of Life

(2) Why Brands Matter

(3) Stephen Bayley

First published in 2017 by Circa Press
©2017 Stephen Bayley and Circa Press Limited

Circa Press
50 Great Portland Street
London W1W 7ND
www.circapress.net

ISBN 978-1-911422-10-5

Printed and bound in Latvia

Reproduction: Dexter Premedia
Design: Flo Bayley

Signs of Life

A PROPOS

My BMW is technologically perfect and in traffic's ugly struggle dignifies me: I become an Ubermensch. My other car is a Porsche and starting the engine, I want to invade Poland. Ralph Lauren makes me look like a Connecticut duke. Nike keeps me fit and Apple makes me creative. Wear a Rolex and my backhand return rivals Federer's. Coke keeps me slim. If I want to be cool, I do Burberry. Sip a Nespresso and – for a tantalising moment – I become George Clooney. Am I a modern hero or a pitiably deluded fool?

Some say that brands are voodoo: sinister spells that perniciously influence the behaviour of individuals, gulling us into paying outrageous premiums for dubious prestige. Others say that brands are our folklore, the symbolic glue that – in our Godless condition – binds us in collective yearnings, providing meaning and value, narrative charm, in a sometimes bleak and threatening world.

'Am I a modern hero or a pitiably deluded fool?'

Maybe. But the individual who created the idea of 'brand management' in 1931 was Neil McElroy, no artist or mystic, rather a one-time Procter & Gamble junior executive who, whizzing through the ranks as whizz kids did, became President Eisenhower's Secretary of Defense in 1957. That year, the United States was humiliated by the Soviet Union beating it into space. The next year, McElroy created NASA's Advanced Research Projects Agency. ARPA later became one of the foundation elements of what we now call the internet. It's not too far-fetched to see a connection here. The idea of brand management was a revolution in business, lionising the intangibles of a product instead of the basic manufacturing function that produced it.

Brand management was about seeing larger patterns in what was already known. So too was the internet. It did not mean the consumer was a stupid dupe, there to be manipulated by junior executives. It meant that the consumer was alive to narrative and symbolism. Brand management recognised the individual's need for identity, just as the internet recognised that same individual's need for the free trade of information.

NASA's rockets took the US brand into space.

The individual who created "brand management" was also
influential in the computing experiments that led to the internet.

Brands are culture, signs of life, evidence that we have moved beyond mere existence-and-subsistence into a world of values and desires. In a great brand, style, symbol and message are all as one. And great brands cheerfully occupy the popular conscious and, indeed, the unconscious. To most people, Volkswagen means more than Deuteronomy. Saying 'Volkswagen' is like painting a picture or telling a story: the name short-circuits cognition to an immediate burst of meaning. And if that's not art, what is?

Of course, this brand world can sometimes be confused, sinister, ridiculous or cynical – Volkswagen certainly can – but it is one that respects the importance of personal taste in civilised life. There are no bad brands since brands only flourish with popular approval: good products create great brands. You cannot make a great brand out of a bad product. The public is not that stupid.

But rules are changing, laws are changing, tastes are changing. The public is changing. Old assumptions about production and consumption are being replaced by new ones. Perhaps one day soon branding will appear as archaic as Henry Ford's manically focused Detroit production lines seem today. The mass production of low-cost identical products supported by global advertising belonged to a very specific historical period, now coming to an end. People today have more choice about how, where and when they engage with goods and services. Or if they engage with them at all.

Now the ties that bind us are being loosened, we can sense more clearly the value in what might soon be lost when brands are outlawed and desire subjected to legal restraint.

❝To most people, Volkswagen means more than Deuteronomy❞

BRAND RECOGNITION

'The intangible aspect of a tangible thing.' Massimo Vignelli (the man who made New York's subways – at last – look smart with modern typography)

'Experiment with and recommend wrapper revisions.'" Neil McElroy (the historic soap salesman who invented brand management with this deathless prose in 1931)

'If I have one life, let me live it as a blonde.' Shirley Polykoff (the brunette woman who realised the world of agonised yearning that existed in hair dye)

'When you get into a car you should feel you are going on vacation for a while.' Harley Earl (Detroit's wizard of kitsch who fully understood the metaphysics of design)

'Coca-Cola is a religion as well as a business.' Robert Winship Woodruff (the man who made Coca-Cola a global megabrand)

'A brand is a promise.' Franz-Josef Paefgen (Audi führer)

'It's all about branding.' Sir John Hegarty (Britain's most successful adman advises his clients on the purpose of life)

'A great brand eats strategy for breakfast; makes the customer look smart; aspires to the condition of music' Stephen Barber (a partner in a Swiss bank who created the Prix Pictet, the world's outstanding photography competition)

Because I think it may be of some help to you in ... Department, ... recommendation for additional men for the Promotion Department, ... outlining briefly below the duties and responsibilities of the brand men.

This outline does not represent the situation as it is but as we will have it when we have sufficient man power. In past years the brand men have been forced to do work that should have been passed on to assistant brand men, if they had been available and equal to the job.

Brand Man

(1) Study carefully shipments of his brands by units:

(2) Where brand development is heavy and where it is progressing, examine carefully the combination of effort that seems to be clicking and try to apply this same treatment to other territories that are comparable.

(3) Where brand development is light

(a) Study the past advertising and promotional history of the brand; study the territory personally at first hand – both dealers and consumers – in order to find out the trouble.

(b) After uncovering our weakness, develop a plan that can be applied to this local sore spot. It is necessary, of course, not simply to work out the plan but also to be sure that the amount of money proposed can be expected to produce results at a reasonable cost per case.

(c) Outline this plan in detail to the Division Manager under whose jurisdiction the weak territory is, obtain his authority and support for the corrective action.

Neil McElroy's 1931 memo : the documentary source of "brand management".

JEOPARDY

There's an awful lot being renegotiated during our continuing post-Industrial Revolution. Mostly, we are becoming dematerialised: all the old ideas about possessions are up for review. "All that is solid melts into air," Karl Marx wrote in *The Communist Manifesto* of 1848 and that turns out to have been his most accurate prediction.

Uber is a taxi company that owns no taxis. The smartphone generation prefers virtual travelling to driving on roads. They even prefer smartphones to drugs: an iPhone satisfies addictive cravings once directed towards speed or dope. Substance abuse is in decline with twenty-something iPhone addicts.

Meanwhile, the old media are dead or dying. Display advertising in newspapers will soon disappear. Maybe newspapers themselves will disappear first. Shops may soon also become things of the past as e-commerce makes the park-and-ride, pay-and-display, out-of-town superstore look as quaint as the high street once did. Certainly, we no longer have a single producer-consumer axis, but many.

So here's another German philosopher. Nietzsche said all of life is a question of taste. And he was right: the choices we make define us. Our possessions define us and sometimes they betray us. Even refusing to make a choice is an irrefragable statement of intent.

Nowadays all of life is also a question of branding. Producer-consumer axes may change, multiply, mutate, morph and evolve. People may still be motivated by desire and magic, by the promises which brands offer, the stories they tell, the secrets they share and the ambitions they excite. Your smartphone tells the time with GPS accuracy, yet you still want an Audemars Piguet, Hublot, Richard Mille, Patek Philippe or a Rolex. Don't you?

So a brand is rather a complicated entity involving many of the absurdities and appetites that define existence itself. A brand is not something concocted by graphic designers and marketing consultants alone, although they play their part. It is a collaboration between consumer and producer in a piece of theatre: playwright and actor working on an agreed script. But the last act is not written.

'All of life is a question of taste'

Brand becomes the expectations and associations which all successful products and services possess. In business terms, it means how much extra people will pay to engage in a harmless directional fantasy. People wanting to enjoy the expectations and associations of Louis Vuitton's portfolio of handbags and champagnes have made the French luxury brand conglomerate worth $28.5 billion.

After soap, cigarettes were among the first consumer products to be professionally branded. Camel, Lucky Strike, Marlboro, Gauloises and Benson & Hedges became a part of global culture. Now, ugly, generic packaging for tobacco is mandatory in the UK. Bans on attractive presentation for sugar, alcohol and cars will logically follow. Possibly, bans on comfortable sofas too because, in certain circumstances, they can inspire deranged lust.

Sinful products will always be vulnerable to reformist zeal. At the same time, the commercial culture that sustains branding is in jeopardy: as conventional advertising becomes redundant, the affluent young flirt with consumer fatigue. In one reading, brands and branding are pernicious, manipulative and in decline. Better, surely, to see them as an economically and culturally precious folk art, which it would be good to preserve.

Too trite a comparison would insult people damaged by smoking, yet puritanical forces similar to those promulgating the *sumptuariae leges*, the Sumptuary Laws of the Renaissance, are behind the generic packaging of cigarettes. Once, in 16th-century Verona, women were forbidden from wearing a low neckline, lest exposed flesh drove youth to frenzy. Elizabeth I's Statutes of Apparel of 1574 were similarly designed to moderate the economic expense of fashionable, but costly, imports and, at the same time, curb the moral decadence acquired from using luxury goods: "the vain show of things" as the Statutes declared.

The needs to forbid and control are at least as human as the appetite to consume and enjoy. The Roman toga *virilis* in its distinctive Tyrian purple was only to be worn after a certain age by men with a certain position. In China, the Confucian notion of restraint created a philosophical disposition towards abstinence. Feudal Japan was strict about clothing and the Quran forbids men to wear silk or gold. True, there was nobility in these forms of restraint, but today, fundamentalist Muslims share with muscular feminists a special interest in wanting things banned. If you Google 'evils of smoking', a vicious Islamist website appears top of the searches.

Generic labelling would diminish the magic of wine.

Indeed, there is a long and depressing history of what is forbidden. And what is compulsory. The vain show of things can be very annoying to the miserable moralist. Forbidding and compelling are two different aspects of the same authoritarian personality, hence the attraction of smoking bans for Nazis. Hitler, while a helpless drug addict injected daily with Pervitin and hormones by his compliant personal physician, was a passionate anti-smoker. However, hypocrisy was the least of his crimes.

Yet banning stuff does not always create social benefit, as Jazz Age America discovered. In 1919, Andrew Volstead's law became the 18th Amendment to the United States Constitution, criminalising alcohol. It created the troubled age of Prohibition with its spectacular crime and lawlessness.

'There is a long and depressing history of what is forbidden,

James Dean made delinquency glamorous.

Similar mentalities are now, rather successfully, exerting control over tobacco packaging. Australia was the first to insist on generic packaging, perhaps the first time the word 'generic' became pejorative. Market researchers determined that Pantone 448C was the ugliest colour in the swatch book and all cigarettes sold in Australia are wrapped in this dingy green-brown. When it was described as olive, the Australian federation of olive farmers made a formal complaint.

The distinguished American libertarian Lewis Lapham says: "I look on the anti-smoking law as a form of sumptuary law. The tax and the oppression, for the most part, land on the poor." And cigarettes retain impressive champions. The painter David Hockney says: "Smoking calms me down. It's enjoyable. I don't want politicians deciding what's exciting in my life." Another great artist, the contrarian Damien Hirst adds: "I smoke because it's bad, it's really that simple." Artists are ever unlikely to be persuaded by conventional anxieties.

Soon, artists may find themselves defending beer and chocolate. If, as many fear, a ban on alcohol and food packaging follows the ban on cigarettes, then a legion of craft breweries and microdistilleries, which have used quality graphics to appeal to discriminating consumers, creating a presence for their emergent brands, will be compromised.

And it is remarkable how illiberal and intolerant the forbidders are: the president of the Royal College of Paediatrics and Child Health, attacking junk food, said there can be "no debate" about the composition of school dinners. In this environment, a child was sent home from school because his packed lunch included a bag of Mini Cheddars, a branded snack product. No debate about the dinner, perhaps, but there certainly can be a debate about branding.

Pantone 448 : research proved it to be the most repellent colour

GUARANTEES AND BETRAYALS

Brands achieve three things. First, a guarantee of quality. Would you rather your money was with the Swiss bank UBS, identified by clean, dignified graphics and centuries of culture, or with Metro Bank, designed to look like a sleazy pound store? Then, unless betrayed, the consumer responds with the second thing: loyalty over time. And as a result of this, that same consumer is less likely to be price-conscious: he will pay more for the promise of quality, reliability and prestige.

An unemployed man was interviewed for the radio while shopping in a supermarket. The interviewee was asked why he was spending money on premium-branded instant coffee rather than the supermarket's own-brand 'value' label. His response was crisp, sure and simple: to buy a value brand, he said, would make him feel poor and disadvantaged.

Fonts create confidence : which looks
the more sober bank ?

SUCKERED BY THE BRAND MEN, OR PLAYING THE GAME?

In this context, value has several different interpretations. In the same way, favela kids who spend $100 on trainers are not being suckered by cynical 'brand men', they are cheerfully participating in a cosmopolitan culture to which their other circumstances deny them access. Who would wish to deny a ghetto child his small pleasures? Brand-weary hipsters might sigh, but in a putrid favela, a Nike swoosh means freedom of expression and confers dignity.

Any attempt to curtail, or even prohibit, sophisticated branding will have a real economic cost in that valuable intangible assets will disappear in a puff of frigid criticism. But it will have a culturally diminishing effect too, draining enchantment, temptation too, from everyday life.

It is noteworthy that the emerging anti-smoking movement of the 60s, so far from destroying cigarette branding, actually enhanced it. In 1965, television ads for cigarettes were banned from British television. Six years later, health warnings were made mandatory on packets. By 1976, actual people actually smoking were no longer allowed to appear in ads. In fact, actual people had been banned from tobacco ads whether they were smoking or not. Agencies were not even allowed to mention the product.

As Sir Joshua Reynolds knew, rules inspire genius rather than inhibit it. An art director at Collett Dickenson Pearce called Alan Waldie began developing cinema and billboard ads for Benson & Hedges, which showed only the famous gold box. In fact, the legend Benson & Hedges was visible, but so myopically that it was not a persuasive factor in the consumer's response to the ad.

One such ad showed a gold box inside a birdcage, with the box casting the shadow of a bird on a wall. Legislators may not have picked up the suggestions of Kafka and of Surrealism here, but consumers certainly noticed. And they responded, Benson & Hedges acquiring a version of intellectual chic.

'Rules inspire genius rather than inhibit it'

Great ads do not have to be rational : an Iguana
worked for Benson & Hedges.

23

ENJOYMENT CAN BE DANGEROUS

The truth here is simple: a great deal of what we do and enjoy is dangerous. The majority of people die in bed. Since 1972 when John Yudkin published *Pure, White and Deadly,* the life-threatening properties of sugar have been well known. The problem is that evolution did not equip mammals to deal with the industrial quantities of sugar we consume: lab tests have shown rats prefer sugar to cocaine, so addictive is it. HFCS, or high fructose corn syrup, is routinely added to low-fat foods to give them taste interest. As a result, the average Briton eats, advertently or inadvertently, about a kilo of killer sugar a week.

Fructose contributes to the accumulation of liver fat and this, in turn, leads to metabolic disease, including diabetes and chronic heart problems. In addition, sugar lowers immunity and compromises the body's use of health-protecting minerals. Then there is the question of sugar's destructive impact on dental health, adrenal fatigue and its contribution to obesity and disorders including eczema and arthritis. They also say it gives you wrinkles. Action on Sugar, a pressure group, says sugar is: "the alcohol of childhood...the new tobacco".

By any reasonable standard, sugar would be banned, or, at least, products containing sugar should be rigorously controlled or, at least, administered to addicts only under strict medical supervision. Certainly, by these measures, there are no good arguments for allowing the manufacture and sales promotion of sugary comestibles.

NECESSARY? WHO SAYS?

Wolfram Schultz is a Cambridge academic who studies the brain's reward neurons: these are neurological elements in the dopamine system that respond to pleasure. They have an evolutionary origin in rewarding our knuckle-dragging ancestors' sensible survivalist choices about what to have for lunch while sauntering across the savannah. Schultz, however, argues that Big Sugar uses garish packaging of sweets and snacks to trigger a pre-intellectual, instinctive response, inciting people to buy 'unnecessary calories' in supermarkets and, later, ingest them while stationary on sofas (perhaps watching soap operas and fornicating absent-mindedly).

Schultz is against any advertising or promotion that encourages consumption of these unnecessary calories. Indeed, he is a firm advocate of using intimidating generic packaging on bars of chocolate, so that ugliness might be a deterrent to desire and taste. However, it is a truth of the retail trade that supermarket own-brand sweets and snacks often come in lacklustre packaging and cost-conscious customers are in no way deterred.

Professor Schultz wants to ban branding so that we will not be seduced by unnecessary calories. This is reminiscent of any authoritarian culture where what is not forbidden becomes compulsory. In cultural terms, Schultz's argument founders on the definition of necessary. Is pleasure necessary? If mere survival is Schultz's end and aim, then we can all do very well eating undressed brassicas, enlivened by the occasional seed and drink water while going to Hell in this joyless way.

Unnecessary sugar is also present in *marrons glacés*, superb Italian *gelati*, chocolate, champagne, Christmas pudding, Château d'Yquem, fresh fruit and many other pleasures, none of which could be considered absolutely necessary in strictly biological terms, but are delightful in terms of civilised behaviour.

Schultz and his tribe of forbidders may not recognise human culture has risen above mere biology, operating with subtlety and nuance.

DE LUXE POLLUTANTS

Cars too should clearly be banned on health grounds. The World Health Organization says one person is killed every 25 seconds in or by an automobile. Every year, about 50 million people are injured in the same way. And the majority of these deaths and injuries are among young or lower-income groups, especially in what used to be called developing countries. As if this lethal account were not already depressing enough, the oil-burning engines in cars generate carbon dioxide, which reduces the blood's capacity to handle oxygen and can be fatal in large amounts.

Then there is NO_x, the various nitrogen and oxygen compounds, which create the smogs that have a devastating effect on global respiratory health. And there is more: the particulates in exhaust gases cause cardiovascular disease and may also be carcinogenic as well as contributing to the greenhouse effect, which is a deadly part of the global warming process.

By any sane measure, the manufacture, sale and promotion of private cars should be banned. And that is even before we consider any of the broader environmental issues, including the automobile manufacturers' voracious demand for metals, minerals and rubber whose provision is raping the planet. Never mind that cars bring convenience and pleasure to billions, on the moralist's profit and loss account, they are in shocking deficit.

Perhaps the day will come when BMWs are sold with health warnings including atrocious pictures of severed heads in autobahn accidents appearing unbidden on the car's infomatics screen. When this happens, chocolate bars will be illustrated with clinical photographs of a struggling 300lb woman being involuntarily fitted with a gastric band. For surely it is wrong to tempt people with pleasures that might damage them?

Will alcohol be next? The evils of demon drink are well understood. Consumed during pregnancy, alcohol can lead to foetal alcoholic syndrome, which often produces disturbing abnormalities. Socially, the intoxication caused by immoderate alcohol consumption produces a huge range of disagreeable social behaviour from wife-beating to public urination and head-butting.

It can also lead to the corrosion of the higher cognitive faculties and has a significant role in public and domestic accidents. Alcohol also has a major and destructive part to play in long-term, life-threatening health problems including heart and liver disease. Psychologically, alcohol creates substantial problems of anxiety and depression. The cumulative economic and health costs of alcohol are ruinous, the justifications of finding a cold beer refreshing, a first growth claret delicious or a glass of champagne a civilised delight are – perhaps – trivial in comparison. Certainly, the anhedonists are against it.

'By any sane measure, the manufacture, sale and promotion of private cars should be banned'

THE CALIPHATE WILL DECIDE

Yu the Great prohibited alcohol during the Xia Dynasty. The Society of Friends, Methodists, Band of Hope Salvation Army and Chartist temperance movement would still like to do so here as well, although progress has so far been slow. However, the coming caliphate may well succeed where the Methodists failed. If you can ban tobacco branding on health grounds, there's no logic that would prevent you banning the sale of first growth claret. Château Lafite might be as stigmatised one day as legal highs are right now. The disturbing conclusion is a future determined by authoritarian interference in consumer choice.

There are rational reasons to question the sense of neutral packaging. While cigarettes are still legal, to interfere with their packaging shows contempt for the rule of law. And there is surely something obscene about autocratic governments appropriating intellectual property. Customs officials know that Australian generic packaging has led to a rise in dangerous counterfeits. When packaging is shared and out of copyright control, what's to stop the unscrupulous imitator? Meanwhile, Australians can be fined AUS$2000 for smoking in public and punitive taxes will raise cigarette prices to the point of inaccessibility, with a view to eradicating smoking entirely in the near future.

The real argument against generic packaging is founded in art, not the political lobby. When the poet William Carlos Williams wrote "No dignity without chromium/No truth but a glossy finish", he expressed much of the pathos of 20th-century material culture, at least as seen from America. The truth expressed by chromium plating may be a real one, but it is based on reflection. All of our modern truths may be forms of subterfuge.

‘ If you can ban tobacco branding on health grounds, there's no logic that would prevent you banning the branding of first growth claret ’

LIES, DAMNED LIES AND
ALTERNATIVE FACTS

And the alarming thing is this: just as legislators are outlawing the agreeable dream world of brands and insisting that cigarettes are sold in pseudo-functional packs with terrifying health and safety warnings, real news is becoming a slippery fiction. One dream world is legislated out of existence while another steps in to take its place. The former White House Communications Director, Sean Spicer has said: "We can disagree with the facts." News is now as readily faked as trademarks once were. We are 'post-truth', Oxford English Dictionary's word-of-the-year in 2016. And 2017's debate about fake news brings new attention to the value inherent in reliable news brands.

When agendas are set by 8chan, The Daily Stormer, Before It's News and Breitbart, all sites that muddle the sacrosanct distinction between news and opinion, reporting and features, a special value attaches to the *Financial Times*, BBC, Reuters and NBC, whose probity and traditions promise quality and impartiality. A better demonstration of why brands matter could scarcely be imagined.

In this contra-factual context it is interesting to note, perhaps a little elegiacally, that Coca-Cola's successful brand message was for many years based on the tag 'The Real Thing'. Written as a barb to its various fake cola-flavoured rivals, this formulation was first used in 1942, but revived in 1969 to signify 'America's rejection of artificiality'. Nineteen sixty-nine, of course, was the historic apogee of the counter-culture. The post-industrial, supra-national, non-aligned, globalised corporation needed its narratives.

Great brands do not lie, even if presidents and prime ministers do.

'We can disagree with the facts'

TOXIC

There's a larger context for the disappearance of old brands and the imposition of generic packaging.

Traditional patterns of consumption and modes of communication are everywhere being tested. And often they fail the test. We are, ever so slowly, approaching the end of advertising, at least as it was understood during the Creative Revolution of the 60s. There are several reasons for this, just beginning with the fragmented media of today and the difficulty that fragmentation causes in accurately addressing markets.

Then there is the decline of print as a medium. Branded content now appears online, disguised as hipster sketches, soaps or even harrowing documentaries. But advertising is under threat because the most important consumers, the young and the rich, simply do not care.

Millennials have become averse to expensive logos on their trousers, even as they commit to fast-fashion brands whose anonymity flatters them with a delusion of being above taste. Conventional advertising is what Harvard's Timothy Wu calls "one more avoidable toxin in the healthy lifestyle". In Wu's analysis, ads are now as dated and repugnant as the obesity products, fizzy drinks and processed food, which they once so successfully promoted.

Today, the cigarette smoker is a rarity, when once she or he was the norm. There are not going to be any challenger brands in cigarettes, no redesigns, no relaunches. Cigarettes are unlikely to be rediscovered: their market is stable or declining. Everything about them is known.

If existing consumers or new recruits are to be deterred from cigarettes, better health education would be a superior remedy to censorious interference with art and design. The threat to the cigarette manufacturers from generic packaging is insignificant, economically speaking, compared to the cultural threat to branding itself.

But on the whole, banning arguments are ultimately weaker than creative ones. Montaigne, sitting alone in his Gascon tower, knew that sumptuary laws were self-defeating, since they stimulate rather than deter because humans are a perverse species. Anthony Trollope said of a 19th-century alcohol prohibition campaign: "This law must fail." It did.

Still, the fear is that generic packaging is not just the last battle in the war against tobacco manufacturers, but one of the first actions in a new and more sinister war against branding itself. And a war against branding is a war against people. Brands are, quite literally, signs of life, or, at least, popular expressions of it. They are culture, art, design, value, belief. And they make a lot of money. Without them, we will in every respect be poorer.

> ❝ Ads are now as dated and repugnant as the obesity products, fizzy drinks and processed food, which they once so successfully promoted ❞

THE COMFORT OF STRANGERS

What good can brands do?

You are staring out of the aircraft window, ruminating on the absurdity of sitting in a 500mph pressurised tube six miles above the earth's surface, hurtling somewhere else. Invisible forces are keeping you there. Strangers are in-charge.

This is like a bad nightmare of Franz Kafka's, but suddenly you notice the Rolls-Royce logo on the engine nacelle. Do you feel better? Of course you do. Rolls-Royce stands for integrity, quality, reliability and confidence... with just the faintest suggestion of unflappable English grandeur. This is just the way you want to feel at FL37. Those are Rolls-Royce's brand values and they are infinitely precious.

There's some dispute about the precise etymology of the modern word 'brand', but what's certain is that the Old Norse word *brandr* meant to burn. A ghost of this meaning is preserved in the term firebrand.

And it became the custom of people who, for example, sold goods in wooden barrels to burn their trademark into the wooden staves. This proved ownership. Additionally, a branded barrel had an identity, which a generic one did not. And, very possibly, it was worth more money as well: perhaps instinctively, we see merit in individual identity and personality. And perhaps we also find fault in the anonymous and the generic. No-one has ever said: "I just met this fascinating person. She's completely generic."

Rolls-Royce stands for integrity, quality,
reliability and confidence...

'No-one has ever said: ''I just met this fascinating person. She's completely generic.''

Thus branding eventually came into currency, as a part of the metaphysics of modern trade, which also include its close relations, public relations and advertising. Branding seems important, not least because it sounds intelligently deliberate, as opposed to the word burning, which carries suggestions of wanton destruction. Branding is an act of will, whereas burning may very likely be negligent.

You branded something to make it your own, to separate it from the mass and to claim your title to it. And in doing this you increased its value. Unfortunately, slaves were branded, as were cattle. But so too were beer and soap, bringing new wealth to their makers and new confidence to the consumers.

All the above notwithstanding, like art, brand can mean pretty much whatever you want. From simple, practical beginnings based in notions of title and ownership, brand has become a vast metaphysical and metaphorical property. Of all the scientific and pseudo-scientific disciplines, which attempt to understand business,

Great brands are burnt into memory.

branding is the one most completely located in the arena of culture and perception.

Asset management, H&R, financial control, holistic book-keeping, R&D, benchmarking are all necessary in an efficient business and they can be managed by numbers. Soon they will be managed by artificial intelligence. Brand is different. It is diffuse, difficult to define, even if the presence of strong brand values are always easy to detect. Brand is about art and imagination, dreams, passion, desire and yearning. Sometimes about lies and deceit as well.

'We work in the dark – we do what we can – we give what we have. Our doubt is our passion and our passion is our task. The rest is the madness of art.' Henry James

None of this has a scientific basis. And that's exactly why it is so fascinating. A successful brand is based on what Henry James described as the madness of art. If it were entirely straightforward to build a successful brand, then everyone would be as rich as Coca-Cola. But because the idea of a brand is not scientific, does not mean it is not professional. While soap may carry a trademark, today even the President of the United States has acquired his own brand.

Actors too. It's notable how the vocabulary of commerce has been acquired by cinema and theatre. While once an actor who misbehaved might have been said to have a 'stain on his reputation', now he is said to have 'damaged his brand'. An actor is no longer someone who learns his lines, gets into character and performs, he is someone who represents a whole hinterland of business activities including product endorsement, licensing, personal appearances, charity promotions and merchandising.

'A successful brand is based on what Henry James described as the madness of art'

In the same way, a film successful enough to inspire a sequel is no longer considered a mere series, but has been promoted to a more impressive-sounding 'franchise'. Sometimes it seems our entire world can be understood in terms of branding.

The marks burnt into those old barrels were trademarks, although such things have existed since long before branding became a self-conscious aspect of business. The process of attributing cash

Hugh Grant under arrest : what once might have been a stain on his reputation became damage to his brand

value to trademarks is often said to have begun in 1900 when the J. Walter Thompson agency in New York published an in-house booklet about trademark advertising. During its own evolution, J. Walter Thompson assisted various clients by creating ideas and images, which still endure in the popular imagination. Toasted cheese and cuddly pets, for example.

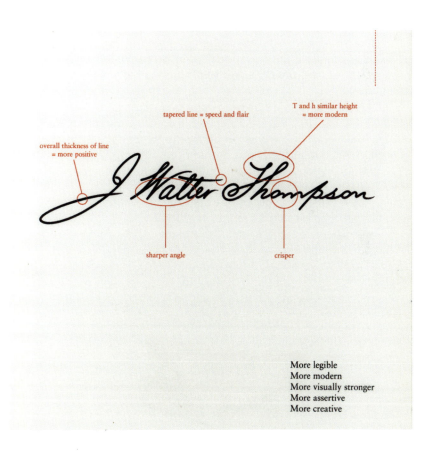

overall thickness of line = more positive

tapered line = speed and flair

T and h similar height = more modern

sharper angle

crisper

More legible
More modern
More visually stronger
More assertive
More creative

Every detail has meaning.

THE REAL MEANING OF A GRILLED CHEESE SANDWICH

While cheese-on-toast had been long familiar and Welsh rarebit can be traced back to at least as early as 1747 when Hannah Glasse mentions it in her *Art of Cookery*, Kraft's grilled cheese sandwich was an invention of J. Walter Thompson in 1930. Thus, through assiduous advertising and promotion, what was hitherto a generic dish became Kraft's corporate property. As if to prove that branding genius is not scientific, 42 years later, J. Walter Thompson decided that a cute puppy was the best possible way to promote what's politely known as toilet tissue.

The original proposal was for a young girl to be shown running through a house, unspooling toilet tissue on her way. This, it was feared, might encourage wastrel behaviour by teenagers, so a Labrador was substituted for a human. The Andrex puppy is with us still, forging a lasting bond in the public's imagination between advanced two-ply toilet tissue and an adorable baby dog. On such curious bases are great brands established: the intangible aspect of a tangible thing, as Massimo Vignelli explained.

Amusingly, however, J. Walter Thompson has been less sure-footed in the presentation of itself. In a fit of acronymic modernismo, it became JWT. No-one liked that much and it soon reverted to the original J. Walter Thompson. Letterheads even showed Thompson's own copperplate signature, as if to suggest antique credibility.

A grilled cheese sandwich
became part of Kraft's identity.

Longest Andrex ever.

Catch this special offer before it runs out.

Andrex has always been very long. But now the best ever value Andrex is in the shops, with more sheets on every roll than ever before.

In fact, this special offer

Andrex is so much longer that it now goes 25% further than just about every other toilet tissue. But hurry.

Andrex may go on for ever, but this offer won't.

Andrex

Soft, strong, and longer than ever.

PUT SOMETHING EXCITING
BETWEEN YOUR LEGS

Every product is more than its mere substance. Every product has become the sum of the messages and imagery that have, by design or accident, surrounded it. In this way, a Harley-Davidson is much more than a motorbike. At first the process of brand-building was accidental: Harleys ran successfully in dirt races, creating one sort of reputation. Outlaw Hells Angels used Harleys, but so too did the police. In California, hot-rod customisers chopped unnecessary parts off the bulky bikes, creating 'choppers'. Dennis Hopper's and Peter Fonda's choppers became the most famous of all in the 1967 *Easy Rider*. All these different associations were enriching to the brand: it's a beguiling paradox that while Harley's reputation is rooted in bad boy culture, the glamour of delinquency, the majority of its customers are middle-aged white professionals.

And then the process became deliberate as 'brand managers' realised they owned an asset – emotional, associational, aspirational – that transcended twin-cylinder motorbikes comprising steel, glass and rubber. They usurped the customisers and began customising factory bikes, as if to canonise heretics. Now Harley-Davidson will sell you apparel and home products, including lawn flags. Whether this will arrest the decline of a business whose customers are becoming extinct, for half a century Harley Davidson was an exceptional example of what *Forbes* magazine called 'social branding'.

Soap, grilled cheese, two-ply toilet tissue, the President and the motorbike all acquired reputations that began with the product, but became more layered and complicated through all the accumulations of meaning provided by years of popular comment, advertising, media exposure and cultural appropriation. Once it was called aura, but now brand has a cash value and a political heft.

The idea of brand has tracked the development of modern business. In a progress that Darwin might have understood, commercial artists of the late 19th century, the poster designers of *belle époque* Paris, for example, evolved into more professionalised graphic designers in the middle of the 20th century.

'It's a beguiling paradox that while Harley's reputation is rooted in bad boy culture, the glamour of delinquency, the majority of its customers are middle-aged white professionals'

A Hell's Angels heritage turns
fund-manager riders into weekend rebels.

BRAND IS METAPHYSICS. BUT THEN SO IS LIFE ITSELF.

And as people began to appreciate, at first slowly, then really rather quickly, that a brand was more than the sum of its tangible parts, graphic designers evolved into branding consultants. They were commissioned not merely to design a trademark or a poster, but to imagine and then visualise a brand. Of course, they had to remain designers too, but their trade was now more subtle, involving belief and yearning as well as typography and illustration. Brand is metaphysics. But then so is life itself.

Brands express (and create) tribal loyalties: although he is not, in the strictest sense, for sale, that is where the President of the United States comes into the branding conversation. Thus Trump's poorly fitting suits and terrible hair make him look like a bad argument, which, of course, he is. If he had a NYSE three-letter ticker, it would be PUS, although he is also formally – and perhaps more happily – known as POTUS. He represents the hopes and fears of the population. JFK did too, but his wearing neat button-down shirts (known in France as 'un Kennedy'), well-cut suits, Moscot spectacles, highly polished Oxfords or neat loafers, all connected to good grooming and a thinking man's haircut, reflected the taste of a liberal elite. Donald Trump's tastes, his brand and his constituency are different.

JFK's sunglasses, like his initials, were an
element of his identity.

> **Thus Trump's poorly fitting suits and terrible hair make him look like a bad argument, which, of course, he is**

Trump Tower : the President-to-be
liked hard, shiny things.

THE LEISURE OF THE THEORY CLASS

Brands involve sensations of belonging, respect, advocacy and sometimes even love. In terms of manufactured goods, since access to technology is now widely democratised and globalised, since bad products no longer exist, the creation of an attractive brand is now perhaps the single most economically important business activity. Thorstein Veblen recognised this over a century ago in *The Theory of the Leisure Class*. As soon as any economy rises above mere consumption, decisions are made on the basis of taste. Or brand.

There is just a quantum of difference between brand and brand values, the latter being the commercial realisation of what was hitherto just observed graphic fact. Brand values are what we used to call 'goodwill', or a business's reputation in terms of the loyalty and respect (and repeat business) paid it by customers. According to Generally Accepted Accounting Principles, goodwill has a cash value. In product terms, it's the difference between what something is actually worth and what someone is prepared to pay for it; that barrel with a trademark burnt into its staves is worth more than a generic one.

And you can do another related calculation to see what that goodwill means: it's the difference between any business's tangible assets and its market capitalisation. The commercial property, the leases, the capital equipment, the cash-in-hand make one figure. The stock market valuation makes a very different one. Try it with, say, Coca-Cola and the answer is that its intangible brand is worth many, many billions.

Putting a shine on brand names.

You can do a similar exercise with Harley-Davidson, Porsche, or any other manufacturer of desirable products. Item: in 1998 Philip Morris paid six times its apparent worth to acquire not Kraft's real estate or factories, but its brands, Kool-Aid and Velveeta, for example. When Kraft – now Kraft Heinz – launched a bid for Unilever in 2017, a bid that would have been one of the biggest in all business history, it was understood not in terms of national champions arm-wrestling, or employment ramifications, but simply as one collection of brands acquiring another.

These intangible assets are supremely valuable: becoming conscious of brands is a way of monetising popular approval. The Harvard Business Review estimated that in the 70s about 16% of the value of the S&P500 index was attributable to 'intangibles'. Today that percentage is in the mid-80s.

> ‘The Harvard Business Review estimated that in the 70s about 16% of the value of the S&P 500 index was attributable to 'intangibles'. Today that percentage is in the mid-80s’

The brand value of Coca-Cola hugely
exceeds their material assets.

PRETEND YOU ARE IN FORTNUM'S

Is there any way of sensing the quality of a brand, or, to use a modish, if grammatically redundant, expression, the brand experience?

Ask yourself how do I know I am in Fortnum & Mason? Well, you will have just stepped off Piccadilly, a fine street with dignity and traditions of its own. And you will have passed a polite, liveried doorman who will have held open the door (with its brightly polished brass fixtures). Possibly, you noticed the Royal Warrants outside, evidence of an established commitment to quality. Inside, people will be very helpful, even if you just buying a bag of crisps. Or how do I know I am in a Bentley? Actually, you easily could tell even if the identifying badges were covered with gaffer tape. There is the solid thwunk of the doors, closing with solemn pressure, the intoxicating clubland aura of diamond-pleated leather. Inimitable. And how do you know this client you are visiting is serious? They serve excellent coffee. These are all as significant in the calculus of brand values as beautiful graphics.

Not seeing the signs : you simply know
you are in Fortnum & Mason.

BUT DO YOU WANT MORE OF IT?

They say that the best test for beauty is: Do you want more of it? If you see something and you want to reproduce it, or experience it again, marry it, steal it, ape it, then it is perhaps beautiful. And, by the same score, ugly is that which is repellent. Ugly is something you very likely want less of. A similar test applies to brands: successful brands generate loyalty and have repeat customers who return to have promise fulfilled, again and again. And that applies to custard as well as to diamonds, as well as to POTUS. It is the engineering of desire. But what is desire?

Desire is a prospector that maps the landscape of all our appetites. It's a radar scan of future possibilities, real and imagined. Desire is yearning with a tangible, but distant, focus. Craving is feral, but desire is cultivated. Craving is what happens in subsistence economies where appetites are very basic. Desire is more sophisticated and sophisticated means are required to excite it.

The existence of desire may even be one of the defining characteristics of civilised life, which is to say: the ability to imagine and project. Desire is not a passive function, but an active one. And it is more subtle and complex than mere lust. Like craving, the latter is crude and unreflective, a spasm of the groin, not a troubadour's romantic strategy, nor the Romantic poet's hard true flame of love. Desire is a function not just of the senses, but of the intellect as well. Lust may (or may sometimes not) be gratified immediately. Desire involves planning.

Desire is always in the future. It is a device for taking you somewhere else. And what excites desire? The smell of tobacco, the ghost of a nipple under silk, the texture of a fresh peach, the sound of a Ferrari, the taste of Krug '09, a sunset over Mont Ventoux... these are so very powerful because they operate in the same neural colonies of the brain where ideas about art and literature are stored. And they are motifs often used in advertising.

‘The existence of desire may even be one of the defining characteristics of civilised life ’

THE SCENT OF A FLOWER WE HAVE NOT FOUND

Then there is the enigmatic nature of desire. C.S. Lewis tried and succeeded in describing it: "...the scent of a flower we have not found, the echo of a tune we have not heard, news from a country we have never yet visited." It's these mysteries that a successful brand evokes: journeys in a BMW will be that much more satisfying, a scented candle by Cire Trudon will turn your bathroom into a Turkish pasha's *bagno*, a grilled cheese sandwich by Kraft does something which a Frigidaire's industrial cheddar never could achieve.

And if this sounds exalting, even religiose, that's not an error. The greatest brands of all, Coca-Cola and Apple for example, actually replicate religious structures. Robert Winship Woodruff, the legendary chairman of Coca-Cola actually said, "Coca-Cola is a religion as well as a business."

'Coca-Cola is a religion as well as a business

SON OF A PREACHER MAN

He meant there is a leader, a product, an eloquent constituency of believers, persuasive imagery, articles of faith. Many of advertising's greatest copywriters came from a Church background: Rosser Reeves of the Ted Bates agency, the man who created the 'Unique Selling Proposition' and explained it in his 1961 classic, *Reality in Advertising*, was the son of a Methodist preacher-man.

Reeves had an idea that business could improve the world: at a loss for how to complete a student examination paper, he wrote an essay called Better Living Through Chemistry. He was perhaps weak on his chemical formulations, but really terrific at occupying the emotional territory, which his lab was experimentally exploring. What's the point of chemistry, unless it makes people happy? Later, Reeves sold that idea and that very copyline to DuPont.

Reeves' central conviction was to separate, in an exegesis that was almost theological, 'image' from 'claim'. He believed in claims. And claims must be absolutely honest. Sometimes, it was very hard work to keep things simple. But if you achieved conceptual simplicity, you often found yourself in possession of a very effective copyline. For example: 'M&Ms melt in your mouth, not in your hand.'

A 59-second ad Reeves made for Anacin headache pills made more money, he said, in seven years than *Gone With the Wind* did in a quarter of a century. Or, at least, that's what Reeves *claimed*. And it was such an impressive one that it is still being repeated today.

THINK SMALL

But Reeves' strict theology did not survive what's been called the Creative Revolution in advertising that occurred in the 60s. His background was the mid-century, Eisenhower years American Dream with three bedrooms, two and-a-half kids, a two-car garage, one wife – who was a dutiful, docile home-maker – and zero anxiety.

The more anarchic pop culture demanded more nuanced, disruptive and culturally suggestive ads. Pop culture needed exciting imagery and critical commentary. It's a glorious paradox that in the anti-commercial context of hippy-dippy 60s counter-culture of hippy fabulousness, advertising was at its very best.

Typical of the Creative Revolution were the Doyle Dane Bernbach ads for Volkswagen. 'Think Small' some of them said. At a time when Detroit was using fabulous air-brushed colour illustrations of its cart-sprung barges with proportions exaggerated even further than reality, DDB used unretouched black and white photographs of challenging (somewhat ironic) humility. Another compared the car with a lemon. These were ironic, confrontational and clever. Many say, not just the best ever car ads, but the best ever ads. They helped make Volkswagen's reputation for reliability, economy and responsibility that was so damaged by the diesel fraud scandal of 2015. But before that, they became iconic.

You should

live so long.

Doyle Dane Bernbach's contrarian Volkswagen ads
used wit and irony to sell an unglamorous product.

EYECONOGRAPHY

Not for nothing does the word 'icon' cross from religion to business to religion and back again. That we use it to discuss everyday goods serves to emphasise the ritual element in consumer behaviour. Indeed, not just advertising, many brands are said, sometimes carelessly, to be iconic.

It was in the 17th century that the word 'iconic' made its metaphorical transition, from religious usage to ordinary speech. In English in the 1650s, 'iconic' began to be used to suggest something that had the status of a painting. It has now evolved into meaning something that is either well-recognised, much-admired or has some synoptic power to suggest a larger value system. In a 2006 survey, Big Ben, a cup of tea, a red phone box of the Scott design, a Routemaster bus and a Spitfire were all said to be iconic. Today, property developers will describe a fashionable loft apartment as iconic, usually irrespective of its true qualities. In November 2016, *The New York Times* carried a headline: "How The Rolling Stones became fashion icons."

There is, however, something more profound to be said about what icon means. Icon, or more properly 'ikon' is the Greek word for a static visual image, most usually in Eastern Christian art. The Orthodox Holy Tradition is inspired by The Holy Spirit and they share access to the Divine Essence: the rhythms of Byzantine poetry are said to have had their origin in the Jewish Septuagint, not Greek classical metrics. Thus, closer to Jehovah than Jupiter.

The very first icon may have been the image of Jesus said to have been owned by Pilate, the prefect of Judaea in Christ's lifetime, but the tradition of making icons only became firmly established three centuries later. This was when the Emperor Constantine's Edict of Milan in 313 tolerated Christianity in the Roman Empire, leading to an increased market demand for religious images: religion and business are forever curiously admixed.

Icons have, beside their astonishing, tranquil, mysterious beauty, certain definable characteristics. One, the image of Jesus tends to be a repetitive one: there was for the Byzantine artist very little scope for psychological interpretation, although several basic types allowed the expression of slightly different gestures and poses. But, essentially, like a brand, the image was firmly established and needed only refreshing from time to time.

Two, icons are objects of veneration often possessing wonder-working properties. Sometimes, icons would weep tears of myrrh. And it was in the genre of icons that the idea of a halo, an aura, first appears in art (and only later got translated into business). Occasionally, icons came into existence in a process known as *acheiropoieta,* which is to say, without an identifiable human artist.

Brands are about loyalty and belief.

STEVE JOBS' DIVINE ESSENCE

An *ikonostasis* is the screen of many icons separating the sanctuary and the nave in an orthodox church: thus, it is the setting for worship. It is before the *ikonostasis* that the faithful say their prayers and do their prostrations. So it might be compared to the annual Apple Worldwide Developers Conference where the late Steve Jobs, possessing his own version of Divine Essence, performed magic.

To what extent it was conscious we will never know, but Steve Jobs' great achievement at Apple was not in technology and design, rather in the creation of a perfect high-tech simulacrum of religion. For a while, this made Apple the world's most valuable company. Apple's cathedral was this Developers Conference, first organised in San Francisco in 1995. Here, in an atmosphere of hushed reverence not at all dissimilar to that of a Byzantine basilica, revivalist meeting or perhaps a more rowdy get-together of snake-handlers in rural Georgia, Jobs presented himself as a messiah-like figure.

The Apple of his i. Successful brands
ape the structures of religion : Steve Jobs'
iPhone became an ikon.

JUST LICK IT

His audience was a congregation of tech-literate faithful who waited for the Word. And, of course, the Revelation. The latter came in the form of exquisitely designed products that commanded slavish devotion. Jobs additionally had a genius for the quotable, throwaway line. He explained to a slack-jawed journalist that you know a design is good if you want to lick it. In this way, Jobs introduced an element of the erotic into the purchase of a smartphone. He made going to an Apple Store a cultured event.

After Jobs died in 2011, the Apple religion was without a leader – at least, without one of the petulant, inspired, charismatic type that Jobs so well represented. So much so that two years after his death, his biographer Walter Isaacson wrote about the Developers Conference he saw in 2013: "The event lacked Jobs' spark, as did the products. [Apple's presenters] used the word incredible so frequently that if it had been the magic word in a drinking game, the launch would have knocked cold an entire fraternity. So many things were described as 'incredible'... that it began to serve as a reminder that none of them really were." True incredibility requires irrational visions and unreasonable behaviour.

When Steve Jobs died, Apple lost that precious asset. But some of Jobs' quasi-religious construct remains in Cupertino. His contrary character – a Buddhist bully, a hippy billionaire, a sensitive sadist – gave people the seductive impression that Apple was a commune of alfalfa-munching, zoned-out, herbivorous philanthropists. That was a subterfuge of genius. Apple is a vast, manipulative, cynical, stock-watching US corporation. For a while, it *appeared* to be something much more attractive. People wanted to believe in Apple. As John Hegarty says: "A brand is the most valuable piece of real estate in the world; a corner of someone's mind."

You have the *ikonostasis* with the Dormition of the Mother of God and Christ Pantocrator or a slickly packaged iPhone 8. In brand terms, their power is identical.

WHAT IS A BRAND?

A brand has to have an unambiguous identity, even if it does not necessarily possess absolutely unique properties.

But this identity has to arise out of special attributes of the tangible kind. Tiffany took legal action to protect its duck egg blue. Chanel has trademarked the scent of its classic No5 perfume. The taste of KFC is proprietary and Lamborghini has patented the unusual scissor-action of its sports cars' doors. Coca-Cola, naturally, protects its famous contour curve.

Or consider shoes. Tod's are immediately recognisable by their *gommini*, the little rubber studs that form the sole, derived from the original driving shoes. Converse All Stars are identified by the five-pointed star. Louboutin has unique red soles and Prada uses an embedded red strip. From these details, all these brands can be recognised without a name being attached.

The smell of success : Chanel has legally protected the scent of N° 5.

You don't have to spell it out : a red sole, a star
and red strip say Louboutin, Converse and Prada.

TIPTREE OR LIDL?

The logo is another element at the source of a brand. Imagine something looking like a Nissan Micra, but carrying the Porsche logotype. What sort of cognitive dissonance would that excite? Anyway, what's a logo? Besides, that is, a debased form of the Greek work for 'word'. And here is another religious association. In Christianity, the Word suggests the infallibility of the Divine. In business, the logo suggests the infallibility of a certain proposition.

Good?

Bad?

A LOGO IS A TRADEMARK THAT WENT TO ART COLLEGE

Anyway, first you have a logotype (which is a designed arrangement of words or letters) and then you have a logogram (which is a designed graphic element), although nowadays they get conflated into the single word logo. Trademarks, we know about. A logo is more highly evolved. A logo is a trademark that went to art college and postgraduate business school.

For a fee of $35 a Portland State University graphics student called Carolyn Davidson created the Nike Swoosh in 1971. The athletics manufacturer was going through a transition. Previously Blue Ribbon Sports, it was decided to rename it after the Greek Goddess of Victory: Nike. The classics have often influenced the design of logos: the ancient Goodyear Tire & Rubber Company logo was inspired by the winged-foot of Hermes, messenger to the gods. Mobil used Pegasus. It's a truism that all great businesses have great logos. And often their history tells little truths about them.

'Previously Blue Ribbon Sports, it was decided to rename it after the Greek Goddess of Victory: Nike'

THE THREE-POINTED STAR AND THE PRANCING HORSE

A badge is not quite the same thing as a logo, but performs an identical function in that it signals the product's identity. The automobile industry is especially rich in badges. The car manufacturers were traditionally known as 'marques', from the French for 'sign', but as their businesses became more complicated, accumulating levels of meaning acquired by generation after generation of advertising, they became brands... even if they were still essentially hardware rather than a mystical collection of signals, associations and expectations. And badges were the point-of-origin.

At the beginning of his career, Gottlieb Daimler painted a three-pointed star on his own house in Cologne as a token of future good fortune. In 1910, it was adopted as the badge of the business he founded: Mercedes-Benz. One of the very first mass-produced cars was the 1903 Oldsmobile Curved Dash model. Its side panels were impressed with the marque's identity.

Rolls-Royce's badge, solemn and classical, appeared in 1906. Indeed, its radiator grille reflected the pedimented front of a Greek temple. It was such a successful projection of values that two years later a Times journalist described it as "the best car in the world". That was not a rational judgement since Rolls-Royce had very many rivals who were at least as competent in matters both of luxury and technology, but as an emotional appraisal it had great resonance. It

BMW's badge uses the colours of Bavarian heraldry and suggests a spinning aircraft propellor.

was repeated so many times that it acquired some of the attributes of truth. Fifty years later when David Ogilvy wrote his memorable copyline about the loudest thing you could hear in a Rolls-Royce being the ticking of the clock, the fact that contemporary Fords were quieter was elegantly ignored. Rolls-Royce had ineradicably become 'the best car in the world'. And that meant the quietest, irrespective of the facts.

Franz Josef Popp, one of the founders of BMW, is usually credited with creation of the famous Bayerische Motoren Werke logo in 1917. The blue and white device of BMW was probably inspired by the Bavarian coat-of-arms, but also nicely suggested a spinning propeller slicing an azure sky. Relevant because BMW first made aero engines which saw service in the First World War. Like all good designs, the BMW logo was capable of development and has consistently evolved for a century, while remaining essentially the same.

The three-pointed star is so strong it cannot
be contaminated by association.

"At 60 miles an hour the loudest noise in this new Rolls-Royce comes from the electric clock"

What makes Rolls-Royce the best car in the world? "There is really no magic about it—it is merely patient attention to detail," says an eminent Rolls-Royce engineer.

1. "At 60 miles an hour the loudest noise comes from the electric clock," reports the Technical Editor of THE MOTOR. Three mufflers tune out sound frequencies—acoustically.

2. Every Rolls-Royce engine is run for seven hours at full throttle before installation, and each car is test-driven for hundreds of miles over varying road surfaces.

3. The Rolls-Royce is designed as an *owner-driven* car. It is eighteen inches shorter than the largest domestic cars.

4. The car has power steering, power brakes and automatic gear-shift. It is very easy to drive and to park. No chauffeur required.

5. The finished car spends a week in the final test-shop, being fine-tuned. Here it is subjected to 98 separate ordeals. For example, the engineers use a *stethoscope* to listen for axle-whine.

6. The Rolls-Royce is guaranteed for *three*

years. With a new network of dealers and parts-depots from Coast to Coast, service is no problem.

7. The Rolls-Royce radiator has never changed, except that when Sir Henry Royce died in 1933 the monogram RR was changed from red to black.

8. The coachwork is given five coats of primer paint, and hand rubbed between each coat, before *nine* coats of finishing paint go on.

9. By moving a switch on the steering column, you can adjust the shock-absorbers to suit road conditions.

10. A picnic table, veneered in French walnut, slides out from under the dash. Two more swing out behind the front seats.

11. You can get such optional extras as an Espresso coffee-making machine, a dictating machine, a bed, hot and cold water for washing, an electric razor or a telephone.

12. There are three separate systems of power brakes, two hydraulic and one mechanical. Damage to one system will not affect the others. The Rolls-Royce is a very *safe* car—and also a very *lively* car. It cruises serenely at eighty-five. Top speed is in excess of 100 m.p.h.

13. The Bentley is made by Rolls-Royce. Except for the radiators, they are identical motor cars, manufactured by the same engineers in the same works. People who feel diffident about driving a Rolls-Royce can buy a Bentley.

PRICE. The Rolls-Royce illustrated in this advertisement—f.o.b. principal ports of entry—costs **$13,995.**

If you would like the rewarding experience of driving a Rolls-Royce or Bentley, write or telephone to one of the dealers listed on the opposite page.

Rolls-Royce Inc., 10 Rockefeller Plaza, New York 20, N. Y., CIrcle 5-1144.

'Fifty years later when David Ogilvy wrote his memorable copyline about the loudest thing you could hear in a Rolls-Royce being the ticking of the clock, the fact that contemporary Fords were quieter was elegantly ignored'

THE IMAGE OF INFLATION

Michelin's Monsieur Bibendum, inspired by a pile of tyres, is not strictly a logogram nor a logotype, but the cheerful personification has become the company's unforgettable symbol and, as a cheerful bon vivant homunculus, a fine, smoking and drinking hedonist advocate of brand values. Monsieur Bibendum was drawn by the cartoonist O'Galop, pseudonym of artist Marius Rossillon.

At first he was a graphic, a poster-boy, but he soon evolved into a company symbol, a representative of emerging brand values. These attractive and romantic Michelin values were established despite the fact that the company's primary product is the very boring car tyre. Bent on pleasure, the smoking and drinking Monsieur Bibendum was never boring.

In 1900 there appeared the first Michelin Guide Rouge, a gazetteer of French towns with driving tips for motoring pioneers and the vital addresses of garages and hotels. For example, the Hotel de France in Montreuil-sur-Mer was given five stars and it was that same town's Monsieur Nivert who could repair your bicycle and pump-up your tyres. A local *garagiste* was annexed to the Michelin brand.

The Guide Rouge was at first distributed free. In 1920, it went on sale and became, and remains, an encyclopaedia of dreams. Just open an old or new Guide Rouge at random and it kick-starts a reverie. The northern French town Maubeuge may in truth be a terrible dump, but Michelin's neat street plan invites you to stroll from the Étang Monier to the Place de Wattignies and imagine that wonderful little charcuterie, bar or bistro you might find. It is suggestive pornography for hardcore Francophiles.

Monsieur Bibendum himself had an ego inflated to a similar pressure as the tyres that comprised him. He smirked, he kicked, he smoked, he drank. He was unforgettable. And he made the Michelin brand.

Tyres are boring, so Michelin created Monsieur Bibendum :
a cheerful, cigar-chomping hominid with a glass always in his hand.

In 1918, an engineer called Nicolo Romeo took over the Anonima Lombarda Fabbrica Automobili, or Lombard Car Company, of Milan. He incorporated the Visconti family's serpent symbol and the word 'Milano' into the badges of his cars and made the very happy coinage of a gloriously euphonious name: Alfa Romeo... which sounds as much like an invitation to make love as the name of an industrial concern.

'Alfa Romeo… which sounds as much like an invitation to make love as the name of an industrial concern '

THE PRANCING LOGO

Enzo Ferrari began his career managing the Alfa Romeo racing team. On his Alfas used as his own badge, a *cavallino rampante* (prancing horse), which he had borrowed from Francesco Baracca, a First World War fighter ace. When Ferrari left Alfa to make his own cars, he took the prancing horse with him. This became the famous symbol of Ferrari, now often cited as the most valuable brand in the world. Meanwhile, when Alfa Romeo began producing cars in its Alfasud factory in southern Italy, it dropped the word 'Milano' from its badge... and the cars lost a little of their identity.

Ferrari's *Cavallino rampante* was 'borrowed' from a WW1 fighter ace.

VOLVO ERGO SUM

Volvo means 'I roll' in Latin. Its logo was created in 1950 by Karl-Erik Forsberg: his idea was to use the traditional chemical symbol of iron, a circle with an arrow pointing out from its north-east circumference, as his point of origin. This happily suggested the product's solidity, but also, at a largely unconscious level, suggested to those willing to see such things, a flash of lightning originating with the hammer-wielding Thor.

These are examples from the early days of the motor industry, when individual manufacturers had genuinely individual identities, but with the consolidation of different factories, a process led by Alfred Sloan when he created General Motors, those identities became blurred. Under common ownership, Oldsmobile and, say, Chevrolet, might begin to share components, diluting the product's engineering personality.

Once established, customer loyalties had to be respected so individual product identities were often retained. The most absurd example of this was when the British Motor Corporation was created in 1952, bringing together Austin, Morris, Riley, Wolseley and MG. Instead of investing much in technology, BMC invested instead in a cynical process that became known as 'badge engineering'.

By about 1960, BMC was offering five different mid-size cars, technically identical, but distinguished by small details, different names and different badges. This betrayal of trust undermined popular faith and BMC began a long and depressing decline into intellectual and financial bankruptcy, which was a melancholy reflection of Britain's own diminished circumstances after 1945.

Be that as it may, British badge engineering was actually established by none other than the peerless Rolls-Royce. When it acquired Bentley Motors in 1931, the product lines began to merge, even if the badges were kept separate. It was correctly recognised that Bentley's winged 'B', an original device of Walter Owen Bentley nicely streamlined by the artist Frederick Gordon Crosby, and Rolls-Royce's 'Spirit of Ecstasy' by sculptor Charles Robinson Sykes were valuable assets. Still, in 1946 the Rolls-Royce Silver Dawn and

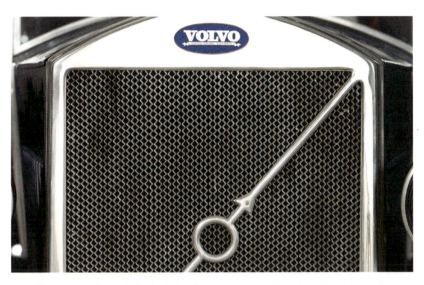

Above: Volvo recruited Thor to help with imagery while
Below: Bentley's flying-B suggested speed and elegance.

Bentley Mark VI with their different badges – were essentially the same car.

Seen from the perspective of, say, 1956, mere badges were the past of branding, but more conceptually well-wrought logos were the future. The logo became an essential part of the work of the new design and strategy consultants, appearing after the end of the Second World War. These, the ultimate realisation of the pre-War Bauhaus ideal of art married to industry, went to work on redesigning not just products, but entire companies.

One of the most influential of these was Lippincott and Margulies. It was Joshua Gordon Lippincott who gave us the term 'corporate identity'. In 1946 Lippincott recast Campbell's soup, not as a mere pantry commodity, but as part of the American way of life. So successful was this positioning that when Andy Warhol later appropriated tins of Campbell's soup into his art, the irony was immediately understood.

'In 1946 Lippincott recast Campbell's soup, not as a mere pantry commodity, but as part of the American way of life '

The real work of art is in the can.

THE TORPEDO THAT SANK

Less successful, but more idealistic, was Lippincott's work with Preston Tucker on the hopelessly idealistic, Tucker Torpedo. This was a car with a bewilderingly odd and advanced specification, which attracted bad publicity because at the launch, the sole prototype could not engage reverse. That ambitious project failed, but after Campbell's, the idea of corporate identity began to emerge and condense, or, at least solidify. Corporate identity promoted art and craft to the theatre of business. It was not just graphics, but a company's entire demeanour and posture – including the quality of coffee served to visitors – which defined the personality the customer understood. Thus, for the Johnson Wax stand at the 1964 New York World's Fair, Lippincott created an environment, which in the carefree usage of the day, would appeal to both 'Hottentots and Eskimos'.

Great US businesses became known by their logos: the celebrity-industrial complex as someone once described it. In 1969, Saul Bass, a graphic designer who had won Oscars for his film titles, made a chaotic and rambling telecoms giant look modern and seem intelligent in brilliant logotypes and promotional films for AT&T. Danne & Blackburn's 1974 logo for NASA made a stuffy federal agency's administration look as sophisticated as its technology.

Danne & Blackburn's made a stuffy federal
agency appear as sophisticated as its tech.

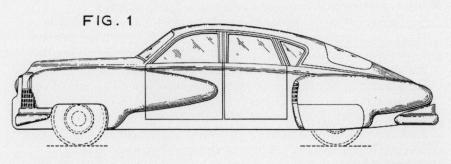

FIG. 1

INVENTOR
PRESTON T. TUCKER
BY
Toulmin & Toulmin
ATTORNEYS

The Tucker Torpedo had everything but a good
reputation and sold only fifty one examples.

AS IF BY MAGIC

The 1994 FedEx logo is outstanding in any survey of the genre. A designer called Linden Leader at Landor Associates, based on a retired ferry boat in San Francisco, was playing around with his two favourite fonts, Futura Bold and Univers 67 and, as he compressed the letterforms, an arrow emerged, unwilled, and as if by magic. Perhaps this was a little like those icons that came into being without the intercession of an artist. It arrests the eye and then occupies the mind. It is not likely that FedEx will ever change it.

It's a fact that creation myths often attend the origin of brands: more evidence of how the very idea of the brand is rooted in mythology and religion. Graphics create enduring images with their clever visual shorthand puns. They introduce a business, but there is something more mysterious, even mystical, behind great brands. A brand is about associations and expectations. The logo is what triggers them. There has to be more to come.

Picasso understood the importance of his personal brand. He soon realised that the given name of Pablo Diego José Francisco de Paula Juan Nepomuceno María de los Remedios Cipriano de la Santísima Trinidad Ruiz y Picasso might helpfully be abbreviated. Thus he became the brand 'Picasso'. Just think, the author of Guernica might have been known as Nepomuceno.

The best graphic accident... ever.

With great artistry, Picasso brand managed himself.

SELLEBRITY

These associations and expectations are possessed by all successful products. According to the American Marketing Association, a brand is: "a name, term, design, symbol or any feature that identifies one seller's goods or services as distinct from those of other sellers." This is something similar to celebrity... in both the good and bad senses. There may be a distinction between celebrity and fame. There is an old line about falling in love with the goddess of fame, but ending up in a one-night stand with the whore of celebrity. Or "sellebrity", as the great adman George Lois had it.

Still, there is no such thing as a great brand which is not famous. Some of the characteristics of the celebrity phenomenon first appear in obituaries in 18th-century English newspapers where the life and works of the subject were often elaborately dramatised.

In his great 1961 book *The Image – a guide to pseudo-events in America*, the Librarian of Congress, Daniel J. Boorstin, a Chicago School intellectual, defined a celebrity as someone who is "well-known for his well-knownness". It's been called a triumph over obscurity, although one journalist attempted to put a metric on it: famous was defined as a matter of being recognised by 80% of the population.

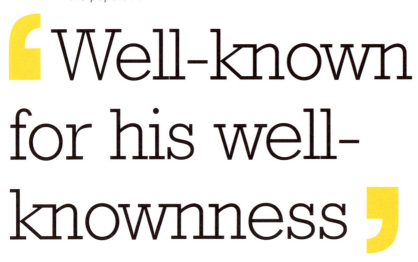

'Well-known for his well-knownness'

Celebrities are brands.

Another journalist, one James Ulmer, established The Ulmer Scale to assess the bankability of Hollywood stars as if celebrities were stock, which, of course, in many ways they are. Today, celebrity, or, at least fame, or possibly even notoriety, are immediately quantifiable by clicks. This very day, George – Nespresso – Clooney has 29,700,000 Google responses to a search. I have 480,000. The point here is that to be noticed is to succeed. Or perhaps to succeed, you need to be noticed.

Great copylines play as large a part as icons or logos in this important getting noticed process. The best ones pass into demotic. Here are some of them:

The New York Times, 1896: 'All the news that's fit to print.'
Adolph Ochs
Camel, 1921: 'I'd walk a mile for a Camel.' N.W. Ayer
Guinness, 1930: 'Guinness is good for you.' S.H. Benson
Kentucky Fried Chicken, 1952: 'Finger lickin' good.' Ogilvy & Mather
Alka-Seltzer, 1953: 'Plop, plop, fizz, fizz, oh what a relief it is. Plink, plink, fizz, fizz.' Jack Tinker & Partners
Mars, 1965: 'A Mars a day helps you work, rest and play.' D'Arcy Masius Benton & Bowles
Hamlet, 1966: 'Happiness is a cigar called Hamlet.' Collett Dickenson Pearce
Braniff, 1967: 'When you got it, flaunt it.' Lois Pitts Gershon Pon
Carlsberg, 1973: 'Probably the best lager in the world.' Saatchi & Saatchi
Heineken, 1974: 'Heineken refreshes the parts other beers cannot reach.' Collett Dickenson Pearce
American Express, 1975: 'Don't leave home without it.' Ogilvy & Mather
BMW, 1975: 'The Ultimate Driving Machine.' Ammirati and Puris
Audi, 1982: 'Vorsprung durch Technik.' Bartle Bogle Hegarty
Apple, 1997: 'Think different.' Chiat Day

WHAT IT SAYS ON THE TIN

These past few pages, written to explain 'What is a Brand?' do exactly what it says on the tin. That was the copyline written by the young London agency Howell Henry Caldicott Lurie for Ronseal varnish in 1994. They branded themselves HHCL. QED.

Successful copylines soon become popular currency.

THE SIGN OF THE TRUE CROSS

There is a ritual element in consumer behaviour.

The Christian Cross was one of the first brands, a symbol by which its adherents were known and its opponents confronted. It had great power, both emotional and practical. And it had the added practical advantage of being easy to apply in all materials and media. Plus, extreme succinctness.

The persecuted Early Christians identified with the Cross and, at the same time, it efficiently projected their values. But it was also a graphic device capable of almost infinite adaptation and development. "It's a logo," John Hegarty says, perhaps a little blasphemously "that's easy to reproduce and is even more powerful when you attach the company founder's son to it."

The Cross was not at first used by furtive and persecuted Early Christians hiding in catacombs, as it too readily reminded them of tragedy and torment. They preferred a fish. Indeed, the Cross incorporating the figure of the suffering Christ appears in art only around the 6th century, 200 years after Christianity became Rome's official religion.

This evolution of the cross happened only slowly, after a lot of hesitancy and false starts. By some accounts, the Emperor Constantine was technically mad (and certainly by inclination a pagan polytheist) when, without any consultative process and with no market research, he chose austere Christianity for his people, many of whom were quite happy worshipping Mithras, the local version of the Persian God of the Sun.

During the early part of Constantine's reign, the Roman Empire was in a wretched state. According to Edward Gibbon's magisterial *Decline and Fall,* Rome was not a calm and dignified imperium but an unsettled mess, divided and riven by competing forces. Gibbon describes "open violence" and "slow decay". So a "pure and humble" religion was able to grow. And the pure and humble Christianity's growth was greatly enhanced by the use of arresting copylines and a brilliant logo. This is how great brands work.

It happened like this. On the night of 27th October, 312, while resting before the Battle of the Milvian Bridge – modern Rome's

Ponte Milvio where young couples now attach love padlocks to lamp posts – Constantine had a vision. It is now surmised that this supernatural vision was, in fact, a large meteorite that crashed to earth at Sirente in the Abruzzo about 60 miles WSW of Rome. A dramatic lake now marks the spot.

The Early Christians understood the power of consistent brand communications, although they started with a fish.

BY THIS SIGN THOU SHALT CONQUER

Still, Constantine, not yet removed from superstition, knew nothing of astrophysics and, instead, saw an impressive aerial pyrotechnic display. Convinced it was a message from the one true God, his soldiers were told to mark their shields with the Christian sign of Chi-Rho, the two Greek letters at the beginning of the word 'Christ'. His army now had its own campaign. And its own logo: *In hoc signo vinces* or By this sign thou shalt conquer. The Chi-Rho appeared as a logo on the military standard, or *labarum*.

When Constantine defeated Maxentius, he felt empowered. The Cross was soon adopted as an instrument to inspire brand loyalty in the new faith. However, a mixture of what Gibbon called "error and corruption", much like any modern media campaign, attended the establishment of Christianity. But a strong copyline and defiant logo turned what was hitherto a clandestine faith of martyrs stuck in catacombs into the world's most influential religion.

As a campaign of information and persuasion, Christianity was exemplary. Adjustment came later, in an especially refined form during the Spanish Inquisition. But early on, it was like a new product launch. From the Jews, the Early Christians acquired zeal and industry. They had a tremendous product offer in the prospect of trademark eternal life, a point-of-difference, a Unique Selling Point, not available to pagan competitors. The addition of show-stopping miracles brought attention and respect.

More-or-less simultaneously, perhaps the very first conscious branding was the Roman Empire's decision to restrict the use of Tyrian purple dye to the cloak of the Emperor. Tyrian purple had been known to the Phoenicians and is mentioned by Homer. It is the colour of clotted blood, according to Pliny and was Cleopatra's favourite. It is extracted from the hypobranchial glands of Mediterranean shellfish whose secretions were fermented in urine before the cloth was added.

A century later, the Roman Catholic Church became another effective branding exercise, effective in all media from architecture

to music: it combined imperial and religious messages. Secular
brands began now to emerge: during the Renaissance, printers'
colophons and paper-makers' watermarks became early brands.
Our ideas about consumer aspirations are by no means all new.

Aldus Manutius of Venice was among the first modern publishers:
his colophon was, of course, an early logo. It comprised a dolphin
wrapped around an anchor, supported by his motto, or what we would
call a copyline, *'festina lente'* (hurry quickly). As if a thoroughgoing

Tyrian purple was exclusive to the Caesars.

corporate identity campaign, Manutius created bespoke fonts for his new printed books. The very idea of *italic* we owe to him. The beautiful modern fonts Bembo and Garamond are derived from his example.

Watermarks had a similar function. They were created by fixing a wire device at the bottom of the mould where the pulp is settling. The pulp takes the impress of the design and the result remains visible in the finished sheet. Literally, watermarks were impressions intended to make an impression. Interestingly, many similar devices, a bull's head and fleur-de-lys, for example, were used throughout Europe. One expert, a Swiss called C.M. Briquet, counted 16,112 watermarks in use in Europe between 1282 and 1600.

Or there was the contemporary example of the *contrade*, or town districts, which compete in Siena's Palio. The *contrade* used colourful branding, often based on animal symbols, to create local identities and establish popular loyalties. Apothecaries began creating distinctive packages for their balms and salves in the 17th century. Many of the bricks used to build the Vatican carry the marks of Antiche Fornaci Giorgi, their maker.

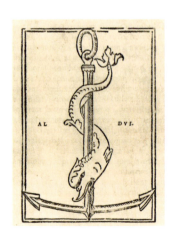

The publisher's colophon of Aldus Manutius
was one of the very first logograms.

The Roman Catholic Church is the very best early example of a complete branding exercise. True, the Christian Cross was already established as a powerful symbol, but its potential was developed with inspired genius and ruthless efficiency. All the elements are there: visual language, consumer experience, a strong revenue stream, great products, loyal people.

The Church was established with articles of faith and it soon acquired numerous believers, created unforgettable imagery and its operatives wore splendid costumes. Global reach was an ambition soon realised and a distribution system was highly refined, dividing consumers between believers and non-believers. Brand values were expressed, as well, in architecture: the Roman Catholic Church understands the concepts of location and presence, building very tall churches on premium city centre sites. Most of the great European cities have at their core a very imposing structure that is, or was, a Roman Catholic Church.

The *contrade* of Siena's Palio use colourful imagery to create local loyalty.

MICHELANGELO,
THE BRAND AMBASSADOR

And, of course, as with all great brands, there was a commitment to quality experience and an extremely persuasive narrative. As for brand ambassadors, you can't do much better than Michelangelo and Mozart. The Sistine Chapel and The Requiem make modern brand promotions appear somewhat feeble. As well as a promise, vouchsafed to the privileged in its famous brand book, The Holy Bible, The Roman Catholic Church had a genius for brand extension: it is active in schools, property, financial services, healthcare and media.

What connects 'eternal life' and 'the ultimate driving machine' is the idea that unwavering belief in one experience, either Roman Catholicism or BMW, will bring that same believer unique and precious rewards. That is the essence of brand: whether a believer or a customer, you invest faith in a belief system and are correspondingly rewarded. And, of course, if the belief system is working properly, the same believers and customers will also become fervent and persuasive proselytisers.

'That is the essence of brand: whether a believer or a customer, you invest faith in a belief system and are correspondingly rewarded'

The Roman Catholic Church and BMW share a commitment to
quality experience with a persuasive narrative.

As nation states emerged in the centuries following the Renaissance, national identity became an issue. Often, countries have been identified with animals, or, in the case of Cambodia, a fruit: the chicken-egg banana being something of a national symbol for the Khmer people. Otherwise, there is the United States' bald eagle and the Russian bear. Australia has its emu and New Zealand its kiwi. France has the Gallic rooster and Iran its proud Persian lion. Britain has a bulldog. Flags achieve a similarly effective graphic shorthand, bypassing consciousness and delivering an immediate sense of a nation.

Old Glory : great brands inspire.

WHAT WE CAN LEARN FROM WALES

The example of Wales is instructive, if only because of the tiny principality's miniaturist obscurity and the bold confidence with which an identity was created for primitive mountainfolk of whom little was understood before about 1800. Even something as subtle, complex and varied as a country can be branded... and rebranded.

There was work to do with the Welsh who have a reputation for truculent independence combined with a diminished sense of joy. They speak a singular and inaccessible language related to Brittonic, which is better understood in Brittany than in London. Perhaps the best we can do for deep Welsh history is to say that Pliny thought the original Celtic priests practiced human sacrifice. A pervasive gloom attends most things Welsh. Poet Gwyn Thomas said, "There are still

Welsh national identity was an invention of the nineteenth century.

parts of Wales where the only concession to gaiety is a striped shroud."

In the 17th and 18th centuries, the antiquarians John Aubrey and William Stukeley made fantastical associations between the Welsh and Druids, which still endure among the uncurious and credulous. Although Bellini's Norma of 1837 is about a Druid, it is rare for the Welsh or the Druids to feature in art. Instead, Druidical imagery is largely an invention of Romantic Era fabulists and fantasists. The Ancient Druid Order was only founded in 1909, the year following the launch of the Model T Ford.

Nonetheless, Wales needed an identity. This new identity for Wales was very much the work of an individual: Augusta Hall, later Lady Llanover of Abergavenny, a formidable woman with a vigorous social conscience, a temperance campaigner, folklore enthusiast and wife the Commissioner of Works, Benjamin Hall who is said, in another chapter of the branding textbook, to have given his name to Big Ben.

Lady Llanover used Llanover Hall near Cardiff (or Caerdydd as Welsh patriots would have it), a nightmarishly fanciful castle designed for the couple by Thomas Hopper in 1828, as the headquarters for her excavation and promotion of Welsh culture. She adopted a Welsh identity as The Bee of Gwent and, although the bardic tradition was in decline, whenever Lady Llanover met an ambitious bard, and one such was Carnhuanawc (who was born as the more prosaic Thomas Price), she cultivated him.

Serenaded by bards, her castle was arranged on supposedly Welsh principles of domestic science and her ideas about Welsh national costume were promoted by suites of watercolours, which she commissioned the better to enforce ideas of Welshness. These were like the mood boards often used in modern presentations where designers show clients the range of colours and associations their new product might acquire. Here we see the 'traditional' Welsh hat, the gown, bed gown, shawl, apron, cape and underskirts. At first, this version of costume was worn for status, but eventually its image seeped into national consciousness: the physical attributes of Welsh national identity had been established. They were modern fancy, not ancient practice, but they helped establish the Welsh brand.

There are still parts of Wales where the only concession to gaiety is a striped shroud

The popular conception of a Druid has no basis in history : it is as modern as Sunlight soap

THE NEW SOVIET MAN
EATS CHEESE

In a different style but with similar intentions, the USSR, a new product launch of 1917, used powerful graphics, publicity stunts and celebrities to create a meaningful, technologically based identity for its bewildered population. They were rallied to action by the prospect of bread and the interesting promise that Comrade Lenin will cleanse the Earth of filth – an attractive corporate objective.

The doctrine of Socialist Realism in art demanded that Soviet male heroes are handsome, always sober, have spotless skin, wear shiny boots and always perform with selfless bravery. A typical title of a propaganda poster would be: 'A Red Army solider grabs the knife in the hand of an enemy dwarf in a Polish uniform, forcing the knife to drop.' That's admirably clear.

REBRANDING JUGHASHVILI

Stalin means 'steel' in Russian and thus was itself an adroit bit of rebranding for a Georgian who was born Ioseb Besarionis dze Jughashvili. There were strict rules about Stalin's representation in art and his clothes were chosen by advisors who were image consultants, except in name. Soviet women were, on the other hand, always blonde and ruddy-faced and cheerful even when driving uncomfortable tractors. Never mind that there is a logical fallacy in the Socialist Realist idea since an image can be either socialist or realist, but probably not both: the effect was mesmerising.

The Soviet System would create a New Man eating his Druzhba (Friendship) processed cheese, wearing his Pobeda (Victory)

The energetic coalminer Aleksei Stakhanov was the
image of patriotic and productive Soviet Man.

wristwatch and driving his Ural motorbike (a BMW R71 copy) to see his tractor-driving Communist girlfriend, avid for Alenka chocolates (which she enjoyed because the wrapper showed a chubby, rubicund Child of Labour, a Slavic Madeleine).

New Man was promoted in art, books, cinema, theatre, lectures and on the agit-prop trains and steamboats that crossed the country in a frenzy of propaganda. One such was Alexsei Stakhanov, who in one record-breaking day in the Kadievka mines, jack-hammer glowing red hot, exceeded his mandated quota by a factor of fourteen, in this way becoming a hero of the Soviet Union. Thus, to be a Stakhanovite was to be driven by the metrics of unusual physical achievement.

Another example was Trofim Lysenko, a pseudo-scientific anti-expertise campaigner who questioned the science of genetics and proposed in its place a sort of agro-mysticism based on "natural cooperation". Never mind that in 1985 *The New York Times* declared Stakhanov to be a hoax and that Lysenkoism became a boorish Luddism, each played a part in creating the irrefragable identity of the Soviet Union. Perhaps it was all a lie, but sometimes lies can tell the truth.

Certainly, the success of Soviet branding created a set of perceptions about Russian power and influence, which still preoccupy the American political and military imagination. True, it was eventually said that much of the US military R&D was spent on projects that did not work to counter a threat that did not exist: graphics were mightier than the sword.

> **It was eventually said that much of the US military R&D was spent on projects that did not work to counter a threat that did not exist**

Stalin knew the word for "Steel" played better
than his birth-name Jughashvili.

THE CUTE SPUTNIK

Space became a new Soviet frontier. Vast engineering projects better satisfied the population's need for symbolism than ham-fisted Socialist Realist painting. Significantly, Sergei Korolev, the chief designer of the Soviet space effort, insisted that his 1957 Sputnik, the first artificial satellite, looked good: the little shiny orb with its trailing antennae soon became one of the 20th century's most familiar symbol. It helped build the Soviet brand.

Later, cosmonauts Yuri Gagarin, Valentina Tereshkova and the space dogs Belka and Strelka all demonstrated what might be called The Left Stuff while in heroic orbit. The choice of the term 'cosmonaut' was significant in that it suggested impressively mystical range. Indeed, the whole cosmonaut programme was founded in ancient Russian mysticism as much as it was fired by rocket science. The very word 'cosmonautics' has a speculative sense, suggesting meaningful philosophical voyages.

Successful, impressive and well-documented Soviet use of space stunts gave a rambling, incoherent, tyrannical union of disaffected and often impoverished nation states the appearance of a potent technological superpower.

With Sputnik and the handsome and personable Gagarin in his Vostok capsule, the Soviet Union for a while bested an aggrieved United States in the matter of popular modern imagery: circling the globe with Soviet graphics is certainly a way of creating brand awareness. *Paris Match* gleefully declared: "The dogma of the USA's technical superiority has been shattered." The humiliation drove the Americans to the Moon.

Kennedy stared at the Moon and saw a promotional opportunity. NASA hired the flamboyant Raymond Loewy. Eventually, a PR man would write Neil Armstrong's unforgettable lines as he stepped onto the lunar surface in 1969. Every event at Cape Canaveral (later the Kennedy Space Center) was televised, creating a splendid branding advantage over the USSR whose Star City was built and managed in furtive secrecy just outside Moscow. The Soviet Union originally branded space, then the United States took over: the dominant narrative of space became American.

'The humiliation drove the Americans to the Moon

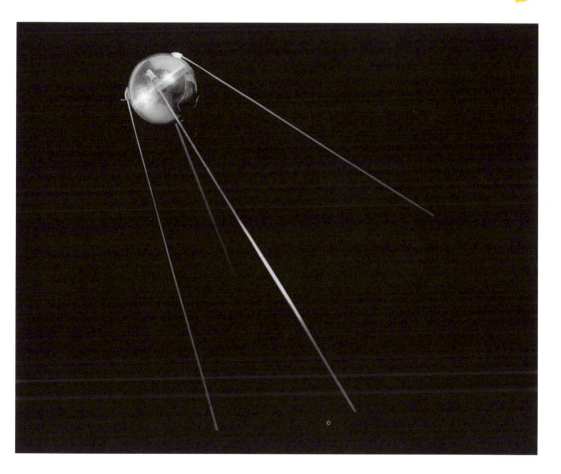

Designers of the Sputnik were
briefed to make it look good

FILTHY, LAWLESS AND OVERPRICED

Cities can be branded or rebranded too. Futbol Club Barcelona was founded in 1899 on a supporters' wave of Catalan nationalism. Now it has a New York office whose opening was celebrated with a party at the Waldorf Astoria where the flag of Catalunya hung next to a fluttering Old Glory. The FC Barcelona brand transcends football: you can buy FC Barcelona Tempranillo wine. *The Times* of London reported that its president, Josep Bartomeu, intended "to burnish the club's global reputation, and then use that reputation to print money".

That's an admirably clear proposition, but city branding can have an ethical as well as mercenary objectives. In the early 70s, New York was culturally, socially and economically depressed. Manhattan, so far from being Lorenz Hart's isle of joy, was troubled by gun-crime and homelessness. Filthy, lawless and overpriced was the word. William S. Doyle, deputy commissioner for the State Department of Commerce, who had lived through the 60s, a decade-long summer of love, when circumstances were more optimistic and less intimidating, had an idea.

He hired the Wells Rich Greene ad agency, whose presiding genius was Mary Wells, one of the first women to smash ballistically through Madison Avenue's glass ceiling, to work on a promotional campaign. In turn, Wells hired the graphic designer Milton Glaser, whose Push Pin Studio had been one of the great image-makers of the age of Pop. Glaser's Woodstock-era poster of Bob Dylan in a fluorescent graphic haze is one the great visual memorials of the age: an icon in the most authentic sense. With a nod to Pop and the prints and paintings of Robert Indiana, Glaser created one of Pop's most popular images.

Indiana had been a pioneer of signs-as-paintings, an adroit and inspired exploiter of vernacular American imagery. A reputation for playing with letterforms led to a commission from New York's Museum of Modern Art for a 1964 Christmas card using the L-O-V-E letterforms. It subsequently became a popular postage stamp and the LOVE sculpture is now in the Indianapolis Museum of Art. And versions of it are in plazas and malls all over the United States.

Indiana said that the angled letter O was either a cat's eye or a memory of an erect phallus, but Glaser's 1977 adaptation of L-O-V-E

Heart direction : Milton Glaser's I-heart-New-York
raised the spirits of a depressed city.

was not so specific. His 'I heart New York' became (and remains) one of the most memorable graphic designs of all time. A rebus and a visual pun, it is the ultimate acknowledgement of how commerce and culture have become blurred. However, Glaser worked on his most successful design pro bono.

New York soon became a safer, friendlier place and Glaser's widely imitated graphic was a symbol of its status as a cheerful world city. The font is American Typewriter, itself a nostalgic design not from the pioneer era of US business, but from 1974.

The next phenomenon in city branding will track the emergence of independent global cities: London, New York, Istanbul and Berlin are becoming separate from their native British, American, Turkish and German root cultures. These global cities have shared supra-national, cosmopolitan characteristics. As crude, protectionist ethno-nationalism infects political life at a country level, global cities will enter a busy, virtuous circle populated by free-thinking cosmopolitans. New York has more in common with London than it does with Nowheresville. Of course, this will make questions of branding and identity even more acute. But we have been here before... with Athens and Rome.

Robert Indiana understood how signs can become art, and vice versa.

'New York soon became a safer, friendlier place and Glaser's widely imitated graphic was a symbol of its status as a cheerful world city'

INDUSTRIAL HERALDRY

Heraldry is an ancient discipline involving the design of coats of arms with special reference to rank, pedigree and status. The Plantagenet arms were: "Gules, three lions passant guardant in pale or armed and langued azure." These three lions were eventually co-opted by the English football and cricket teams. But between the Plantagenets and the First XI, brands became the heraldry of the first Industrial Revolution.

Before centralised mass-production in factories, everyday commodities, beer and soap for example, had been made within geographically precise communities and consumed within the locality: you would actually know the name and identity of the person who made your stuff because he was a neighbour. Advertising was unnecessary because there was little competition. Distribution was not a problem as your source was in walking distance. Marketing was irrelevant because choice was limited.

But industry atomised that old system: consumables and goods were made in faceless factories remote from the places they were bought and used. They were now distributed from afar and required identities so as to be recognisable and memorable. This change from anonymous, hand-made commodities consumed locally to mass-produced branded goods distributed widely is one of the defining characteristics of the modern world.

Good logograms, including the Plantagenet
lions, work in different contexts.

THE APPLE OF STAFFORDSHIRE

Josiah Wedgwood of Burslem in Staffordshire was a master potter, inventor, industrialist and retailer. He was the first modern marketeer, the Apple of his day. Wedgwood had advanced product, employed artists (including John Flaxman and George Stubbs) as product designers, published a sales catalogue and used canals, the most sophisticated delivery network of his day, a watery internet.

Additionally, he was an impresario of his product. Wedgwood put his masterpiece, a copy of the Roman Portland Vase (a promotional piece of which he was especially proud) on display at his Greek Street showrooms in Soho, selling tickets so that the public could marvel at his genius and, possibly, be driven towards an interest in his more modest products.

Like Apple's campus in California, Wedgwood created an ideal community at Etruria: here progressive architecture and a form of social utopianism spoke of corporate purpose. Wedgwood said: "I saw the field was spacious and the soil so good as to promise ample recompense to anyone who should labour diligently in its cultivation." The use of the word "saw" proves that his was a mind of vision.

> ❛I saw the field was spacious and the soil so good as to promise ample recompense to anyone who should labour diligently in its cultivation❜

HAPPY WORKERS ARE
GOOD WORKERS

Wedgwood's neighbour, Bass of Burton-upon-Trent, founded in 1777, became the first branded beer. A century later in Cheshire, William Hesketh Lever sensed he could acquire greater customer loyalty if he gave his soap a name. Lever was the son of a wholesale grocer in Bolton, Lancashire. Long before the company he founded became the huge multinational Unilever, he realised the importance of branding and of social responsibility.

Lever's genius was directed with special attention towards the creation of soap. There were other soaps available in late 19th-

Sunlight soap was among the very first branded products : ads emphasised wholesome solar energy.

century Britain, but Lever's was unusual because he insisted on natural ingredients and, with equal vigour, branding. He called his product Sunlight since it was redolent of nature and wellbeing. Its manufacture was outsourced until 1886, when he built his own factory. And for the workers in his factory he created a model village.

Port Sunlight was built on what Nikolaus Pevsner called an "unpromising" site on the Wirral Peninsula. It was bleak and marshy, with three tidal creeks running down to the stinking River Mersey and Liverpool beyond. Nature's shortcomings were relieved by inspired architecture. Port Sunlight was part of a long British tradition of improving the conditions of Marx's downtrodden proletariat. Cadbury's Bournville in Birmingham was another example. But it also drew on the artistically important picturesque tradition: its pleasant red-brick houses recalled the Arts and Crafts of William Morris, although there were Flemish touches too. Villagers were given allotments and, eventually, an incongruously grandiose Lady Lever Art Gallery.

The village centre was designed by a student from Liverpool University's School of Architecture and Civic Design (which Lever had also founded). And when the first 28 houses were finished in 1890, Ebenezer Howard had not yet published his influential tract about the Garden City. That was to come in 1898 and gave rise to Letchworth and, ultimately, to Milton Keynes.

Port Sunlight is a part of the history of the ideal city, which can be traced back to Plato, but there was more to this than pure philanthropy: Lever believed that happy workers were good workers. In Port Sunlight, you can positively feel the radiant benevolence given off by the architecture and absorbed by its inhabitants: it was a Potemkin village that actually worked. Lever also anticipated the customer magazine when he began to publish the house journal *Progress* in 1899.

Wedgwood, Bass and Lever were all distinctively British enterprises, inspired in equal parts by their proprietors' sense of paternalist duty as by a modern commercial vision. That was to be realised elsewhere when the second Industrial Revolution occurred in the United States. Here migration from country to city was even more exaggerated in its psychological effects than in Britain.

MEGA!

The majority of rural Americans were rootless first or second generation newcomers – from Sweden, Germany and Italy – removed from their old native culture, but lacking any real attachment to a new one offering emotional relevance. They needed symbols of belonging and, satisfying this appetite with a cocktail of lofty genius and cynical hucksterism, the great brands grew into national franchises, which gave this diverse, immigrant population a sense of belonging on a vast, foreign continent. From this beginning, Coca-Cola, Hertz, Howard Johnson, Wells Fargo, McDonald's and, eventually, Nike all grew to national and then global prominence: megabrands.

Packaging began to be fully understood as a sales tool in the 1920s – at exactly the same time that four-colour magazine printing became available and radio advertising was inaugurated when KDKA in Pittsburgh began commercial broadcasting in November 1920. Roads and railways expanded simultaneously. Accordingly, business used road-side architecture to promote brand awareness.

And colour played its part in this architectural branding: White Castle restaurants had distinctive crenellated pseudo-medieval sheds

HoJo's red roofs were instantly recognisable
on the highways of mid-century America.

in the Midwest and Atlantic coast. White, it was felt, suggested pleasingly high levels of hygiene. Howard Johnson acquired exclusive rights to cater on the New Jersey and Ohio Turnpikes where its orange roofs were immediately identifiable. In 1954, HoJo went into lodgings with the same distinctive orange.

During this same period, pioneer industrial designers Walter Dorwin Teague and Raymond Loewy made, respectively, Texaco gas stations and International Harvester service depots recognisable because of striking red-and-white or yellow identities. And both companies' brands were enhanced because these same public buildings were designed in an agreeable and easy-going form of American *modernismo*, gently suggestive of useful progress without the disruptive suggestion of revolutionary intent that attached to the European Modern movement, which was its source.

Indeed, it is one of the great curiosities of 20th-century culture that the radical programmes of the European architects and designers were best realised not in the socialist USSR, but in capitalist corporate America. Architecture as an element of corporate branding has, over the years, enhanced the visibility and credibility of Chrysler, Sears, GM, AT&T, Citicorp and Donald Trump.

DELICIOUS, REFRESHING BRAIN TONIC

But in any account of the story of branding, Coca-Cola is the real thing. Its epic business system was the ultimate franchise: a nearly perfect money mechanism opening-up the American Dream to thousands of businessmen and, of course, millions of consumers all eager to participate in a simple-minded fantasy. Only in a vast country where major companies demanded rapid distribution everywhere could franchising develop. This was largely Coca-Cola's invention: distributing its precious syrup to independent bottlers while protecting their interests, as well as the customers', with a potent brand.

Before it became a religion,
Coca-Cola was a medicine.

There was something touchingly and distinctively American about the franchise system as it evolved in the early 20th century: those isolated rural communities with disparate ethnic origins were not even connected by telephones, let alone interstate highways or airlines. The easy connectivity of today was unimaginable. With no state religion and very little history, a brand represented a belief system, a fixed point in a vast and rapidly evolving New World: in this reading, the religious aspect of the brand again becomes obvious. Southern Baptists may wince at the blasphemy, but it is often said that, after the Christian cross, Coca-Cola is the most recognised logo in the world.

It was Coca-Cola founder J.S. Pemberton's bookkeeper, Frank M. Robinson, who had the happy idea of naming the product after its principal contents. Originally 'The Ideal Brain Tonic', Coke was not at first so very different from snake oil or other patent medicines sold at country fairs. But it did contain natural ingredients: the coca leaf, or traces of it, and the kola nut. With an immortal inspiration, the 'k' became a second 'c' and, written in Pemberton's copperplate, this became Coca-Cola. It was Robinson who added 'delicious and refreshing', so he became the author of one of the best ever copylines.

A logo and a copyline anchored all this entropy into something of certain value and predictable quality. But there was a problem with the way it was sold. Because the Coca-Cola business model was based on the distribution of a concentrated syrup which was carbonated by resellers, its precious identity was confused and compromised by bottlers from Vicksburg to Birmingham creating their own glass packaging.

In 1910 one of them decided: "We need a new bottle, a distinctive package that will help us fight substitution... we need a bottle which a person will recognise as a Coca-Cola bottle even when he feels it in the dark. The Coca-Cola bottle should be so shaped that, even if broken, a person could tell what it was." So in that modest memorandum was the germ of the most successful ever package design and the birth of the planet's first and greatest megabrand.

'After the Christian cross, Coca-Cola is the most recognised logo in the world'

THE SEXIST BOTTLE

An approach was made to the Root Glass Company of Terre Haute, Indiana, whose Swedish plant superintendent, Alex Samuelson, had the happy conceit of using the drink's main ingredients, the coca leaf and kola nut, as inspiration. This gave us the bottle's infamous Callipygean curves, so-called because of the resemblance to the shapely bottom of the famous Venus of Callipygos (a Roman copy of a Greek original now in Naples' Archaeological Museum) and the distinctive flutes. These contours, part-vegetable, part-erotic, became a defining element of the Coca-Cola brand.

You can hold the contour bottle with just one hand. Decades of advertising this simple fact was used to demonstrate Coke's position in American life. Drinking from the neck of the bottle was not uncouth: it was the American way. It was the way to drink for a nation always on the move. Thus, Coca-Cola was a fundamental expression of American culture at a certain moment. The European cup and saucer required two hands. These were for sedentary cultures committed to long drawn-out social rituals, but Coke was dynamic.

The designer Raymond Loewy once said that the Coke bottle reminded him of the shapely Venus Callipygos.

There was even formal advice on how to drink from the bottle with decorum: "Place the topmost sterile ring of the opened bottle lightly against your lips – avoid putting the neck of the bottle in your mouth. Now part your lips slightly to permit free entry of air into the bottle – avoid closing lips on bottle. Then tilt your head and bottle together – Coca-Cola flows freely into your mouth."

Thus, Coca-Cola provided a 'delicious and refreshing' pause during a day's hard work at the face of the Work Ethic. Management, even senior management in their charcoal suits, posed for corporate photographs gripping six and half ounce bottles.

A Coca-Cola president once said: "Basically anybody can make a drink... The reason for our success is... the atmosphere of friendliness we create." Advertising and design helped turn a carbonated beverage with herbal extracts into a global necessity. But it was a promotional initiative of the Second World War, something perhaps to do with wanting to be liked, that inspired Robert Winship Woodruff to say that every man in uniform can get a Coke for a nickel, "regardless of how much it cost the company".

'Basically anybody can make a drink… The reason for our success is … the atmosphere of friendliness we create'

A NECESSITY OUT OF SUPERFLUITY

───────────────

Andy Warhol had a special understanding of Coca-Cola, which like BMW, never deviated from a single proposition. Warhol especially enjoyed, even if a tad ironically, the democratic appeal of this drink: a single product appealing to everyone. In 1975's *The Philosophy of Andy Warhol he writes:* "You can be watching TV and see Coca-Cola, and you know that the President drinks Coke, Liz Taylor drinks Coke, and just think you can drink Coke too. A Coke is a Coke and no amount of money can get you a better Coke than the one the bum on the street corner is drinking. All the Cokes are the same and all the Cokes are good. Liz Taylor knows it, the President knows it and you know it."

The great achievement here was described by Coke's rival Pepsi. "No-one needs it!" Yet in the United States more people choose a carbonated beverage than water. As *Forbes* magazine said of Hallmark greetings cards: "create a necessity out of superfluity". That, of course, is what many great brands do.

BIG SOAP INVENTS
BRAND MANAGEMENT

───────────────

It was at General Motors in the 20s that Alfred Sloan, a figure in the history of American capitalism equivalent to Marx in the history of Communism, recognised what was later to become known as 'brandscape'. That's to say, each of GM's manufacturing divisions had a very specific appeal to a certain part of the population: you could progress from a blue-collar Chevrolet to a white-shoe Cadillac without ever ceasing to be a GM customer. For Sloan in 1927, Harley Earl created car styling to give symbolic form to the market differentials.

Brandscape was altogether more sophisticated than the cynical badge engineering that occurs when manufacturers were unable to offer original products with real appeal. The notion of construing the entire US marketplace as one whose ambitions and tastes could be understood in terms of the five-car division of General Motors might have been merely audaciously absurd, had it not for a while been so very successful and attractive.

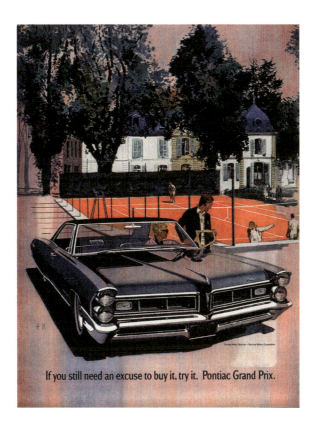

If you still need an excuse to buy it, try it. Pontiac Grand Prix.

General Motors' brandscape identified precise
socio-economic groups : Pontiac customers
played clay-court tennis and lived in houses with
Provencal shutters.

FURS AND STATION WAGONS
OR MONEY AND BRAINS

The proposition, based on the notion that the drama of human life could be enhanced by access to ever more material goods, was that you began your career with Chevrolet and, as your circumstances improved and your horizons widened, you might graduate to Pontiac or Oldsmobile, with their own subtle distinctions of meaning. As you became truly prosperous, you might choose between a Buick or a Cadillac, depending on whether you were a country-club type or a more urban plutocrat. The accuracy of this evaluation of US society was confirmed by Coca-Cola who as recently as the 80s was still referring to particular markets as 'furs and station wagons' or 'money and brains'.

For a brief moment, coinciding with America's hegemony over the world's morals and resources, this brand-determinism stimulated one of the most gloriously vulgar episodes in the history of design, enriching General Motors and enchanting the consumer simultaneously.

The backstory is illustrative. Henry Ford's "any colour so long as it's black" was not an attempt to restrict consumer choice. It simply referred to his company's preference for painting Model Ts black because, in the days when painted cars were put in the sun to dry, it was fast and therefore cheap. But by the mid-20s, American consumers were beginning to want a little flair. When General Motors provided it, one of the biggest ever adventures in popular taste began.

The manipulator was Harley Earl, one of the most influential people who ever lived. Earl was the impresario of the American Dream, great adjuster of the consumer's cupidity, chief wizard in the glorious den of kitsch that was General Motors in the 50s, capitalism's cunning alchemist. It was Earl who created automobile styling. Amazing to say, before he started GM's Art and Color Division in 1927, no-one, and certainly not Henry Ford, had realised that a car's appearance was essential to its desirability. Nor that the same appearance created awareness of the brand.

DUFLUNKY, RASHOOM AND ZONG

In money terms, Earl was perhaps the most successful designer ever, but he never actually drew a thing. Instead, he created moods and directed opinions. He seduced the public with epic vulgarity. He garbled English magnificently. One of his famous instructions to a cowering underling trying to draw a Pontiac detail was: "I want that line to have a duflunky, to come across, have a little hook in it, and then do a rashoom or a zong."

'I want that line to have a duflunky, to come across, have a little hook in it, and then do a rashoom or a zong'

It was once calculated that with all the available variations of colour, body style, engine, transmission and trim specifications, at one point in the 50s the Chevrolet Division of General Motors could potentially produce more automobiles than there were atoms in the universe, thus putting Harley Earl one step in front of God in the chain of command. Blasphemy apart, Earl understood the public's deepest yearnings and instructed his thousands of designers to make absurd machines, which teased their cupidity.

An element of this was the extraordinary illustrations, which Art Fitzpatrick created for GM's Pontiac division. In the history of meaningful deception, these are at least as impressive as the dazzle paint of Great War battleships. When other manufacturers were using photographs, Pontiac used lasciviously gorgeous airbrush fantasies where, crucially, the proportions of the cars were exaggerated for dramatic effect. And their settings showed romantic coves, yacht clubs or golf clubs: the geography of suburban desire. "You get in a car," Earl used to say "and you feel as if you're going on vacation for a while." As an act of persuasion, this was majestic.

And then there was soap. If General Motors in Detroit realised how the design of products could direct and reflect personal taste and desire, it was Procter & Gamble in Cincinnati who first codified the theory and practice of the brand. In 1931, Procter & Gamble realised that the brand of its soap – championed by its 'brand man' – was at least as valuable as the fat and oil it was made of.

As an act of persuasion, majestic.

Image in this way for the first time surpassed substantial reality. This was one of the great metaphysical transactions that still define contemporary life and gives brands their quasi-religious aspect.

The pioneer brand man was Neil McElroy. An internal memo written by McElroy on 13th May 1931, as a bid to get more staff for the promotions department, has become a part of branding folkore. In it, McElroy is very anxious to establish and dignify the role of the brand man. He must study shipments and analyse why some products succeed and others fail. And he can learn from failure as well as from success: he must look at the advertising and speak to dealers as well as consumers. He must be relentless in pursuit of sales: here his short horizons help improve his view. Then he must develop a properly budgeted plan: bottom-line drivers were always a priority, but he must also be scrupulous about copy and crucially "experiment with and recommend wrapper revisions". That thought let a little creative light into the practice. It has to be admitted that McElroy did not think over-much about ethics or sustainability, but nor did most business people in the 30s.

OVERTURE; THE SOAP OPERA

At the same time that McElroy was making brand management a new business discipline, Procter & Gamble began to sponsor radio drama. These were aimed at what were then called housewives and became known as 'soap operas'. This creative expansion of a product's reach into theatre by sponsorship brought with it useful associations of romance, drama and comedy, emotional elements not always associated with detergents. Procter & Gamble even created its own production company to make broadcast soaps, a process that ended only in 2009 by which time completely new media were offering more effective ways of enlarging the territory of its brand values.

BRITISH RACING FAG PACKET

But between 1931 and 2009, there were other notable corporate sponsorships. Most exceptionally, it was in 1968 that Colin Chapman persuaded Imperial Tobacco to sponsor his Grand Prix racing cars. At the Spanish GP of that year, Graham Hill's Lotus 49 appeared in the exact livery of a pack of Gold Leaf cigarettes. Hitherto painted a patriotic British racing green, a Lotus in red, white and gold suggested that national interests and associations were less significant on the global stage than corporate ones.

At the same time, this cigarette sponsorship suggested that sport itself was now being construed as a medium through which brands might be promoted. Lotus changed its sponsor to John Player Special, and the radical Lotus 72 appeared in dramatic black and gold livery at the beginning of the 1972 season. Lotus then switched sponsorship to Camel, while rival McLaren won backing from Marlboro with the cars, most memorably of Ayrton Senna and Alain Prost, wearing paint jobs immediately evocative of a Marlboro pack. Thus skill, speed, glamour, bravery (and perhaps even danger) were added to Marlboro's existing brand values.

More recently, the Red Bull energy drink has acquired an entire, successful Formula One team, winning four world championships with Sebastian Vettel. This is part of Red Bull's commitment to extreme sports, including aerobatics, aircraft racing, space adventures and cliff diving, which help turn a carbonated delivery system for caffeine into a belief system... and a powerful brand that has annexed adventure.

One hundred and seventy seven years after it was founded by two enterprising British chemists, Procter & Gamble understood itself as a corporation of brands. In order to clarify its way of doing business, in 2014 it divested itself of over a hundred brands, leaving it with a core collection of 65. These included Ivory, Ariel, Crest, Gillette, Oral-B, Tide, Vicks, Tampax and Flash. Twenty-one of Procter & Gamble's brands had annual sales of more than a billion.

While P&G has been supreme in the management of its portfolio of branded products, it has on occasions been less successful in managing its own corporate reputation, at least so far as trademarks were concerned. There were recurrent media stories in the 80s that the traditional corporate logo employing the moon and stars were satanic symbols, inspired by references in the Book of Revelations. The Church of Satan, expert in these matters, denied any involvement.

Brandscape established an alternative reality for consumers. You did not buy a mere car, you bought the ultimate driving machine. You did not buy a mere Coke, you taught the world to sing in perfect harmony. Your cigarette made you feel like an Arizona cowboy, even in Leeds. Your hair dye lets you get the very best out of life: "If I have one life, let me live it as a blonde" as the brunette Shirley Polykoff so

Wrapping a Formula One car in cigarette livery was the most audacious promotion ever

unforgettably and plangently wrote for Clairol. Guinness was good for you and happiness was a cigar named Hamlet.

In a personal act of brand extension, Neil McElroy became US secretary of defense on 9th October 1957, just days after Sputnik 1 went into orbit to do service for Soviet brand values. In February the following year, McElroy established ARPA (Advanced Research Projects Agency) and sponsored the Polaris missile for the Navy as well as the Atlas and Titan missiles for the US Army.

Atlas and Titan were later used as manned satellite launchers for NASA as the agency caught-up with the leading Soviet space programme – or 'closed the missile gap' in the language of the day – while ARPA was one of the agencies that created the internet. In 1959 McElroy left government and returned to Procter & Gamble as chairman. In this remarkable brand man, soap and space travel were equally significant.

Procter & Gamble created the original
soap opera

'If I have one life, let me live it as a blonde,

THE ULTIMATE SELLING MACHINE

But there is a lot of misunderstanding surrounding brands. If they are signs of life, sometimes they can be intimations of mortality too.

Brands can't just be created: they have to evolve. The people who created BMW didn't sit around with their cheroots and steins of beer in a Munich office in 1919 and say *"Ach, Fritz, wir mussen eine grosser Weltbrand machen, hein?"* Instead, they simply got on with the job of making the best possible aero-engines, motorbikes and (much later) cars. This they did with absolute conviction. And with absolutely consistent (and beautifully aligned) engineering and artistic philosophies. With excellent ads to support it all.

BMW never deviated from this. They never even made commercial vehicles, let alone messed about with dubious brand extension into incongruous or irrelevant products. BMW's advertising has always been consistent. It has always charged premium prices and invested hugely in R&D. As a result, BMW became one of the most potent brands in the world. All successful car brands behave in the same way.

WOULD YOU BUY A CAR OFF A MAN WHO KEPT PIGEONS?

And then there was Tesla, the first viable electric car. Significantly, in terms of aesthetics, its designers decided to ape the conventions of the established luxury sector. So, the brand message is confused: drive a Tesla and you buy into some virtue-signalling because of clean electric power, but you do not want to lose your hold of more antique forms of status – a Tesla looks very much like a Jaguar, a Lexus or an Audi. Still, Tesla represents a new approach (even if the cars are manufactured in an old General Motors plant). Many consumers who have no idea about Nikolai Tesla find this attractive.

He was obsessed with a 'Death Ray' that would transmit electricity and believed that flexing your toes increased your IQ

Nikolai Tesla's rotating AC induction motor is a thing of wonder, making a magnificent job of converting electrical energy into propulsive mechanical energy Tesla was, himself, out there in the blurred margins of sanity. He said his eyes had turned blue because his brain was used so much. He was obsessed with a 'Death Ray' that would transmit electricity and believed that flexing your toes increased your IQ. Additionally, he kept pigeons in the New York hotel room where he led a life of well-publicised chastity. Would you buy a car named after this man? Many do.

WHY MARX WAS RIGHT

But not everyone shares this reverential view of branding or sees it as a prosperous type of folk art. Wally Olins, much influenced by the example of Gordon Lippincott, became Britain's most articulate spokesman for corporate identity during the last two decades of the 20th century. In one of his books, he declared that brands are the most significant gifts that commerce gave to popular culture. The hard-left critic Terry Eagleton – author of *Why Marx was Right* (2011) – disagreed: "Olins may regard being manipulated as a gift, but not all of us share this psychological kink."

BRANDED BOXERS

The whole business of branding, in Eagleton's view, was "as nastily dehumanised as a workhouse" and offers only a spurious sort of freedom to the consumer, which "now lies in deciding which particular set of grubby deceptions to resist". As for Olins himself, Eagelton said he "only knows who he is because of his brand of underpants".

That maybe the sort of remark that says more about the author than the victim. Eagleton's polemic had been anticipated by Naomi Klein's 1999 bestseller *No Logo* which, hypocritically, used a very strong jacket design to establish its brand. Besides, history does not record if Eagelton wears no-brand underpants or, possibly, no clothes at all in a principled decision to move around the world unlabelled and bravely uncompromised by mercantile capitalist swine. But he does make one fascinating remark when Olins' method is compared to Karl Marx's.

The Wally Olins view of culture was based on the notion that the modern consumer is alienated from identity and meaning, so must seek these values in manufactured goods. Then there is the phenomenon of 'reification', how objects define us. And last, related to the former, is the commodity 'fetishism': the excessive veneration of what Marx would have called brands if only he had had access to the word. That this comparison works rather well is eloquent not only of the validity of Marx's original insights, but of the profound, essentially humane nature of brand culture.

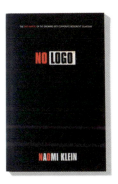

Invisible man : even unseen underwear has brand values to support a man's personality. Invisible woman : the hard hitting graphic paradox of No Logo.

TORCHES OF FREEDOM

In one sense, cigarettes were a defining consumer commodity: a product of the industrial age, at once unnecessary, but desirable. Cigarettes, like soap, are mostly the same – tobacco, humectants and paper – and need branding to create desirable character. From the beginning, cigarettes, like soap, were sold with evocative names of rivers, wildlife or plant life.

R.J. Reynolds' Camel, for example, was preceded in the manufacturer's brand portfolio by Old Rip, Fat Back and Red Meat: its idiosyncratic and evocative graphics by Fred Otto Kleesattel of Louisville (whose company Klee Ad Art also created the Four Roses Bourbon identity) addressed a fashionable taste for Egyptian cigarettes and helped define a new product.

You did not buy a packet of cigarettes, you bought a pack of Camels. That a beast notorious for bad temper and insanitary habits (it is a common fear among hypochondriac travellers that Camels have congenital syphilis) became the beloved emblem of a successful brand simply proves that consumer behaviour is rarely rational.

Larry Rivers *'Beyond Camels'* of 1980
was an ironic take on Klee Ad Arts original
Egyptian themed pack design.

SHOW ME YOUR
CARTIER SUSPENDERS

Camel's success was closely watched by R.J. Reynolds' rival, George Washington Hill of the American Tobacco Company. At first Hill thought Camel a "joke", but nonetheless went looking for a suitable brand to develop. He did not have to go far: in 1871 the American Tobacco Company had registered 'Lucky Strike' as a name for pipe-smoking plug tobacco. Like 'pay dirt' and 'cheapskate', the expression 'lucky strike' came from the Californian Gold Rush of 1849. This same Gold Rush also, indirectly, brought us Levi Strauss's blue jeans, whose tough construction was admired and enjoyed by the miners.

Luckies were test-marketed in Buffalo in 1916 and went on sale nationwide the following year. The ads said, "It's toasted". In fact, all cigarette tobacco is toasted. Instructively, early ads showed a piece of toast pierced by a fork. In pursuit of Camel's market leadership, in 1923 a skywriting campaign spelt out 'Lucky Strike' at 10,000 feet above 122 American cities. There was a permanent exhibit at the corner of New York's Broadway and 45th Streets and the Lucky Strike Radio Hour debuted on NBC in 1928. This programme gave us the term 'hit parade' and was later presented by Frank Sinatra.

‘ Like 'pay dirt' and 'cheapskate', the expression 'lucky strike' came from the Californian Gold Rush of 1849 ’

REACH FOR A LUCKY INSTEAD
OF A SWEET

There were other celebrity endorsements. Claudette Colbert said Luckies were good for her throat. In the same style, Princess Marie of Romania had endorsed Pond's Cold Cream. Pioneer woman aviator Amelia Earhart was enrolled to the cause. Luckies were presented as slimming aids: in the days when such things were possible, ads showed a fat black woman eating candy on a street corner while an elegant white woman who was smoking whooshed past in a limo. Copyline: 'Reach for a Lucky, instead of a sweet.'

Even before its 'iconic' redesign, Lucky Strike had been co-opted into US popular culture. The pack had appeared in a painting by Stuart Davis in 1921 (now in New York's Museum of Modern Art). Davis was a pioneer American modernist who had exhibited, as a very young man, with Matisse and Picasso at the influential Armory Show of 1913 which introduced America to the latest European fashions in art.

In 1921 Stuart Davis became one of the very first artists to incorporate a brand into a painting : "I paint concrete, American things" he said.

PAINTING AMERICAN THINGS

Lucky Strike chimed with him since his artistic engagement was with the modern world and the realities of a commercial and technological society. He painted spark plugs as well as cigarettes, adapting the language of ads to the techniques of painting. "I paint America," he said. "I paint concrete American things." Lucky Strike was proto Pop before it actually became Pop.

Hill met the designer Raymond Loewy in 1941. They shared a certain crass flamboyance. Hill showed off his Cartier cigarette case, Loewy responded by twanging his Cartier braces. They bonded. The two had been introduced by veteran adman Albert Lasker of the Lord & Thomas ad agency, who said of Hill: "I would not call him a rounded man. His only purpose in life was to wake up, to eat, to sleep, so that he'd have the strength to sell more Lucky Strikes."

To this end he taped Lucky Strike packets to the rear window of his

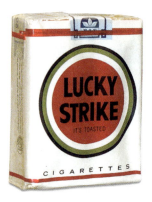

Classic graphic : Raymond Loewy's
re-design of Lucky Strike.

Rolls-Royce and named his dogs Strike and Lucky. He also wore, to business meetings, a battered fisherman's hat festooned with hand-tied flies and an angler's lures. He was pugnacious and beyond parody. Edward L. Bernays, Freud's nephew and a pioneer of the public relations profession, described him as explosively aggressive.

With Loewy as the designer and Lasker and Bernays giving advertising and PR back-up, a magical act of transformation was achieved in the presentation of Lucky Strike and this became a classic study of design effectiveness, Loewy replaced the traditional pack's green – whose ink carried a bad smell – with a more pleasing white. All subsidiary text was removed to the sides of the pack and the red target enlarged and used on both the broad faces: the double logo was genius. Like Donald Deskey's contemporary packaging for Tide detergent, it suggested, no matter how misleadingly, *cleanliness*.

Raymond Loewy's taste in packaging
infiltrated both bars and bathrooms.

It has often been said that circa 1950, the average American could spend his or her entire day in contact solely with branded consumer goods of Loewy's devising: a branded existence being one realised version of the American Dream. A Schick razor and Pepsodent toothpaste in the morning bathroom rituals, a ride to work in a Studebaker or a Greyhound bus. Once in the office, a little work with the Gestetner duplicator, a Coke from the dispenser and a beer after work. Plus, of course, a cigarette.

Soon after Lucky Strike came an even more remarkable cigarette brand. Marlboro was launched in the US by Philip Morris in 1925, although a brand of the same name had existed before in Britain. Marlboro was sold at first as a genteel 'lady's cigarette': you could even buy them with red tips to disguise revealing lipstick traces. A *Vanity Fair* ad of 1926 said: "Marlboro cigarettes have found a place of honour in pockets and handbags in almost every club and community in the United States." And it added: "They lend charm to smoking." But sometimes charm is not enough.

' Circa 1950, the average American could spend his or her entire day in contact solely with branded consumer goods of Loewy's devising '

Torches of freedom? Mel Ramos. Before
feminism, women were routinely exploited in
cigarette ads. As well as in cigarette art.

TONY THE TIGER AND
MARLBORO MAN

Professionalising a 'relationship with the consumer' is a defining part of modern business, even if the coordinates of the practice were understood in the Renaissance. Many ads created relationships through personification, not all of them sophisticated. And a leader in adding anthropoid aspects to fast-moving consumer goods was the Leo Burnett agency. They gave us the Jolly Green Giant, the Pillsbury Doughboy and Tony the Tiger, an amiable felid who, in some weird logic, was thought fit to represent Kellogg's breakfast cereals.

And it was Leo Burnett who in 1955 created the Marlboro cowboy. Because there had been some success in selling Marlboro to women, the filter cigarette was seen as effeminate. And in the historic moment that Tom Wolfe called "America's Bourbon Louis Romp", effeminacy was felt to be a disadvantage. So, to appeal to male smokers, a new, more rugged set of Marlboro imagery was created, employing types not usually seen with handbags.

At first, sailors and construction workers were included in the Leo Burnett campaigns, but the cowboy soon began to emerge as the beau ideal of butch independence, of tough, indomitable loners with cowpuncher's wrinkles scrutinising the horizon of their destiny through squinting, sunburnt eyelids in a haze of Virginia tobacco smoke somewhere on lathery horseback in Arizona.

Leo Burnett's line was: "The cowboy is an almost universal symbol of admired masculinity." To that end, the first models were a US Navy officer and, perhaps a little incongruously, an agency art director. Eventually, Fate decided that Clarence Hailey Long, a real-life cowboy from the JA Ranch in Amarillo should become Marlboro Man. But Long, in his faded blue denim, chaps, Stetson and bandana, was not in fact a complete media innocent. He had appeared in *Life* magazine in a 1949 series about ranch culture. For Marlboro, the cowboy offered helpful associations, although the ads did not, of course, explain that cowboy Long was, in fact, a Baptist who refused to endorse beer. Nor were his views on feminism especially advanced: "If it weren't for a good horse, a woman would be the sweetest thing in the world," he said.

Meanwhile, Marlboro became, perhaps, the world's outstanding branded product. In 1963, the Marlboro Man television campaign used Elmer Bernstein's theme from The *Magnificent Seven,* thus bringing new elements of cinematic heroism and derring-do to the brand's existing sun-tanned rawhide, steely firm-jaw associations. Long's successor was Darrell Winfield who, while anonymous, became the most familiar image of a man in the world.

The novelist Walter Kirn described the almost ecstatic feeling of using an American branded product in surroundings which the ads had made to feel 'natural': lighting-up a Marlboro Red in the Grand Canyon, or driving a Jeep across an arroyo seco, for example. That's a relationship with nature too. And it rather shows that the experience of great brands can enhance even dramatic reality.

Marlboro Man : smokers are real men.

POP, ADMEN, MAD MEN

When packaging became a part of painting's iconography, the place of brands in culture became secure.

It was British artists, suffering under a regime of grey skies and brown soup, who discovered the allure of America's polychrome commercial culture in the 50s and invented Pop. Eduardo Paolozzi and Richard Hamilton made art out of trade, exploiting well-known American brands as visual shorthand for a world of pleasures beyond their immediate reach. A tear sheet from a pulp magazine, a misappropriated piece of packaging, the image of a Coca-Cola contour bottle all could assume the status in contemporary art that saints had enjoyed in earlier centuries.

In the United States, Andy Warhol, Ed Ruscha, Tom Wesselmann and Larry Rivers were among the artists who created some of the most memorable 'icons' of the contemporary moment, treating commercial labels, Campbell's soup, Brillo soap pads and, of course, Coca-Cola, as art, or inspirations of it. While these pictures of cream of tomato are purposefully derived from commercial originals, their lasting impact suggests that great brands can be read at many levels.

From Paolozzi to Warhol, Coca-Cola has been
a short-hand for The American Dream.

THE CARTOON NIPPLES OF THE AMERICAN DREAM

And there were of course, cigarettes. Wesselmann shows desultory nude smokers with cartoon lips and nipples, while Rivers gave cigarette packs the allure of art – *Pink Tareyton* in 1960, *Disque Bleu* in 1961 and *Beyond Camels* in 1980 form a remarkable sequence of images, which hint at the resonance these brands had for gallery-goers. Rivers' *Beyond Camels* reached $425,000 at a Christie's sale in New York in 2013. In 1962, Rivers' painting *The Friendship of America and France* set his takes on French and American cigarette labels in an emblematic tableau, a satire: a commentary where a cigarette brand becomes a metonym of a state.

This fusion of high and low culture was a characteristic of the period Matthew Weiner immortalised in *Mad Men* where everyone smokes and drinks, where suits are sharp, grooming precise and morals loose. Referring to the series, George Lois, a real-life model for Don Draper, told *The New York Times* in 2009: "It was intelligent. It was sharp. It was irascible. It was thrilling. It was cultural provocatism... Back then there was this driving passion. It was like a crusade. Everybody knew something important was happening. We were changing the culture of America."

‘Everybody knew something important was happening,

Tom Wesselman and Larry Rivers were Pop
Artists fascinated by brands and smoking.

THE BEST THINGS ON TV

Unlike Britain, where television grew out of radio, in the US, television grew out the movies. And in this way advertised brands acquired some of the persuasive force of cinema: the Clio Classics ad awards of the 50s and 60s were Alka Seltzer (1953), Marlboro (1955), Pepsodent (1956), Clairol (1957), Crest (1958), Hertz (1961) and Ajax (1963). That list is a version of contemporary culture at least as persuasive as Pulitzer's journalism or Pritzker's architecture.

It was the great admen (and women) of the 60s – George Lois, Bill Bernbach, Mary Wells – who shaped popular television (while helping to popularise modernism in architecture and design, a theme which gave Weiner's series so much of its dramatic force and visual fascination). In 1966, Stanley Kubrick said: "Some of the most imaginative film-making, stylistically, is to be found in commercials."

Gas bored : the 1966 re-brand of Mobil
included graphics and architecture, imposing
global uniformity.

By about 1970, the best things on television were the commercials.

Never mind Big Soap, Big Oil had even more use for branding. In 1966, Mobil initiated the world's first consistent campaign of global corporate identity, transforming its every single filling-station on the planet to architectural designs by Eliot Noyes, a student of Bauhaus-founder Walter Gropius, with graphics by Chermayeff and Geismar. Never had there been such global reach in any branding campaign.

CHESTER GOULD VERSUS ROY LICHTENSTEIN

Tom Wolfe has been the best observer of brands in the last half-century. Indeed, his literary style has sometimes been-called a laundry-list approach to description where the evocation of a single brand name can suggest, or sink, a character's personality. At the same time, Wolfe was fascinated by how during his lifetime, vernacular and commercial art had usurped fine art in its power to exalt us. He wrote an essay called 'Chester Gould versus Roy Lichtenstein', whose argument leads to the conclusion that the commercial illustrator Gould is, in fact, a superior artist to Lichtenstein, the man he inspired.

In the essay, Wolfe writes about the Phillips Petroleum branding with its '76' logo appearing on very visible illuminated orange globes throughout Los Angeles. This he saw as a work of art much superior to contemporary gallery contents. The '76' globes were by that same Raymond Loewy who had transformed Lucky Strike.

To Tom Wolfe, Los Angeles' familiar
Philips 76 globes had the resonance of art.

SO HOW DO YOU MAKE A GREAT BRAND?

You start with a good product. There is no such thing as a mediocre product becoming a great brand.

Then, great brands are created by great graphics and advertising, consistent storytelling and – most importantly – associations which consumers find attractive. As well as religion, they have the characteristics of heraldry and mythology too. People enjoy brands because they have meaning. And it's a pleasure both to enjoy and to subvert them: how exactly to interpret when you hear someone say "He's the sort who wears Ralph Lauren shirts"? Well, it tells you that Ralph Lauren is a brand with real meaning.

YOU WOULD PREFER NEATNESS

An architect called Eliot Noyes, Harvard-trained by the Bauhaus émigré Walter Gropius, gave IBM's Thomas Watson Jr. the most concise and inspiring bit of corporate guidance ever. Watson, who had met Noyes while flying army gliders in the Second World War, asked his friend what he should do about the sprawling, uncoordinated variety of buildings, products and graphics made by the founder of the computer business. Aghast at the mess of it all, Noyes said: "You would prefer neatness."

So for IBM, Eliot Noyes, in chinos and natty bow tie, devised one of the most complete corporate identity campaigns of all time. This turned a gigantic and even sinister component of the military-industrial complex into one of America's most friendly and familiar brands. Noyes hired another Bauhaus émigré, Marcel Breuer, to design elegantly confident modernist buildings. Paul Rand, himself rebranded from the Peretz Rosenbaum he was born as, did the graphics. They remain fresh nearly 60 years on.

Noyes himself designed neat new products, including the *Mad Men* era IBM electric typewriter. And, to get a wary public familiar with the reality of computers, Noyes put some humming and whirring mainframes into the vitrines of Saks Fifth Avenue. He painted them a startling colour and, ever since, IBM has been known as 'Big Blue'. So successful was Noyes in achieving a dominant reputation for IBM, that when Apple began its own influential brand-building campaign in 1984, it used Ridley Scott to make ads casting the older company as a sinister, Orwellian Big Brother.

THEY JUST DID IT

Great brands also need great lines. And they can come from unexpected sources. "Let's Do It" were the celebrity murderer Gary Gilmore's last words before a Utah firing squad in 1977. Copywriter Dan Wieden tweaked this to 'Just Do It'. And they did.

But as they say in Zen, whatever is true, the opposite is truer, so, ironically, Mujirushi Ryohin which, better known as MUJI, sells 'No Brand Quality Goods' all over the planet. And the brand is immediately identifiable by high-quality, sealed plastic wrappers the products are sold in.

And related to the anti-brand brand is the anti-corporate corporation: Virgin and South West airlines position themselves as bold outsiders, even when capitalised in the billions. Most especially Apple whose most successful exercise in positioning is to have created the aura of being an anti-authoritarian commune of alfalfa-munching hippies, while, in fact, it is an enormous, cynical and manipulative corporation whose secretive and obsessive way would have brought discredit to the Machiavellian General Motors of the mid-50s.

Paul Rand's IBM logo suggested the traces of a cathode-ray-tube.

POST-COITAL TRISTESSE FOR THE SPIRIT OF ECSTASY

Brands are certainly signs of life, but sometimes they become extinct. Or contaminated. When in early 2017 Rolls-Royce plc (which manufactures turbines) was involved in a bribery scandal and the shit hit the turbo-fan. Rolls-Royce Motor Cars, an entirely independent company since it was bought by first Volkswagen and then BMW had to issue a disclaimer. The black-and-silver double-R, the Spirit of Ecstasy mascot, the Pantheon grille on the cars themselves were not, its press office implored journalists, to be used to illustrated stories about the jet-maker's corruption trial.

Muji is an abbreviation of the Japanese for "no brand". It is, of course, nothing of the sort.

KICKS HELL OUT OF A HUMVEE

Can there be better – or worse – evidence of the power of brands than ISIS's attraction to the Toyota Hilux? Who has not been impressed by news pictures of white pick-ups in a murderous conga-line on the Syria-Iraq border?

It's a dreadful footnote that ISIS has learnt so much from Western media techniques, but queasily fascinating that it takes such pride in ownership, pride that would not be out of place in Westchester or Surbiton where radical Islam does not flourish. Even more fascinating that someone is art-directing these propaganda images with all the skill of an infidel adman.

Somali pirates also have a strong preference for the sturdy Hilux. It's the ride-of-choice for lawless killers everywhere. These questions were boldly fielded by Toyota. While properly disdaining associations with bigotry and savagery, the company took pride in the fact that the Hi-Lux's reputation for reliability is understood and appreciated by customers everywhere. Even those who want to retro-fit a Soviet-era DShK heavy machine-gun onto the flat-bed.

Indeed, interrogated on the matter of utility and robustness by a diligent reporter from *The New York Times*, a US army ranger said the civilian Toyota "sure kicks the Hell out of a Humvee" (referring to the Army's clumsy AM General High Mobility Multipurpose Wheeled Vehicle).

Sir James Frazer, the pioneer anthropologist whose 1890 masterpiece, *The Golden Bough,* is one of the richest sources of deconstructed myth, had an explanation. Frazer gives us the concept of 'Sympathetic Magic', which is based on notions of similarity and contagion or, as he put it: "like produces like... an effect resembles its cause". Or put it this way: you are your car.

'It's the ride-of-choice for lawless killers everywhere'

ISIS Video

UN-BRAND

Brands may create value, but they can destroy it too. How many potential Hi-Lux owners have been deterred by ISIS?

But there is another sort of brand contamination, a matter of negative associations and low expectations accumulating from successive commercial disappointments, popular betrayal or technical failures. Xerox, Kodak, Polaroid and SAAB are typical and may never be revived. Wary that idiosyncratic book-lovers distrusted its corporate brand, in 2017 Waterstones began to open new stores, which concealed their identity and appeared to be independent.

It is often reported that millennials, a global mini-tribe that used to be called 'young adult consumers', disdain logos. And it is certainly true that in the West there is widespread disenchantment with consumerist excess, while in China the same phenomenon occurs because consumers are embarrassed about shows of wealth in a regime that is, at the same time, becoming vigilant about corrupt back-handers. Johann Rupert, whose company owns Cartier, expressed his confusion to *The Washington Post:* "This is really what keeps me up at night... people with money will not wish to show it."

And just as Harley-Davidson struggles with its shrinking demographic, so too does Levi's. No-one wants a 'dad brand'. Not even dads want one. And was it just dim management and truculent unions that prevented Royal Mail from becoming a FedEx? Perhaps it was a lack of a good logo: sometimes , you need more than Royal associations. Is it taste or legislation or redundant ideas that makes some brands fail while others endure? Can Coca-Cola survive obesity outrage and the stigma of sugar, the alcohol of childhood?

'This is really what keeps me up at night… people with money will not wish to show it'

MARKS & SPENCER CUSTOMERS ARE FAT

Sometimes, organisations commit suicide. SNCF, the French national rail company, spent nearly forty years promoting its TGV as a reliable, advanced, high-speed train. Then in 2017 it threw away this valuable acronym to rebrand the service "InOui" which sounds very similar to the French word for boredom.

Why did Marks & Spencer, once unassailably secure as a Great British Brand, never become a Cos or Zara? According to John Hegarty, it is because Marks & Spencer lacks a "philosophy". As recently as the 90s, M&S was on *Vogue* covers, but there soon followed ruinous advertising campaigns including one whose purpose was to demonstrate the retailer's unprejudiced reach, its acceptability to women of all sizes and tastes. Instead, theses ads were read as meaning 'Marks & Spencer customers are fat'.

Desperately, management invented the new proprietary brands of Per Una and Autograph, but they failed to halt the historic decline in clothing sales. The reason? No-one believed in them. You cannot invent brands. Like culture itself, they develop slowly.

At their best, brands are inspiring, which is why people who do not actually drive a truck will wear a baseball cap with the legend 'Detroit Diesel'. It is why people who have never been to Manhattan say they love Milton Glaser's New York. It is why Vetements can sell someone who is not a courier a DHL T-shirt for $266. In Cambodia, you can buy Alain

After more than thirty years promoting the *train à grande vitesse* as a high-tech transport system, SNCF rebranded with a homonym for boredom.

Delon cigarettes. Whatever the sector, brands offer dreams that are accessible. And, of course, sometimes dreams and nightmares are indistinguishable. Association and expectation are part of the consumer's response to any brand, but so too is recollection.

Marketeers are forever attempting to measure the way consumers remember things, often employing bogus methodology and impressive, but meaningless, numbers. John Hegarty has complained that marketing people "are in thrall to technology, not ideas. Technology enables opportunity, creativity creates value".

And that creativity is more a matter of perverse whim than laboratory experiment. In any case, a high measure of the 'recall' that so preoccupies market researchers does not necessarily mean a high level of acceptance. We remember horrors very well indeed. Still, as Hegarty says: "Better be known for something than be forgotten for nothing."

Instead, the way great brands sediment themselves in our imagination tells us something about the way memory operates in culture. The art of memory was a matter that fascinated Renaissance thinkers: one schema was to imagine the plan of a memory palace with an idea left in every room. To recall a complex set of ideas, just take your mind on a walk around the memory palace. And memory was, of course, the inspiration of Proust's masterpiece *À la recherche du temps perdu*. Proust beautifully called it *"l'édifice du souvenir"*.

Deliver us from folly : Vetements will sell someone who is not a courier a T-shirt costing $266.

ATTENTION FARMING

This is exactly what a brand does: perform like a souvenir, forming a lasting impression in the consumer's memory. Brands operate in that large an interesting area between literature and fridge magnets. They succeed not just by winning our attention, but securing it and working on it. Referring to the media's lust for your eyeballs, Harvard academic Timothy Wu has called it "attention farming". But it's a useful expression for all consumer behaviour. And attention farming is getting more difficult in a distracted age. Millennials, dazed by the delusions and vanities of self-expression, do not want logos.

But then nor do a lot of more mature consumers. In 2017 Bottega Veneta was running an advertising campaign whose transgressively megalomaniac theme was 'When the only initials you need are your own'. To be sure, no logo is visible on a Bottega Veneta handbag, but the brand is readily identifiable from the unique style of *intrecciata* woven leather. No matter how much people may think they flee from identity, they can never escape.

One anti-logo millennial, interviewed by *Women's Wear Daily* said: "I just bought a pair of fake Doc Martens because I really don't care." Absurdly, that showed that she did care. Her apparent denial of brand affiliation is in fact a reaffirmation of it since it's obvious that no-one would bother to fake anything that was not attractive in the first place. And then to boast about the conscious acquisition of a fake? But who wrote the rule that consumers have to be rational?

" I just bought a pair of fake Doc Martens because I really don't care "

IS HISTORY TOAST?

Watermarks, trademarks, logos, advertising and brand culture have all followed the evolution of modern business. Now this culture is under threat from disaffected millennials and radical reformers. Maybe a long adventure in business iconography is coming to an end. Maybe brands are history.

A refusal of brand culture by younger consumers may well be an accurate reflection of a world where immateriality is more substantial than stuff. People don't want stuff any more, they just want an iPhone. A fashionable rejection of acquisitiveness finds its equivalent in Airbnb, the world's biggest hospitality business, which just happens not to own any properties. There is a metaphor clamouring to escape here.

There are unenchanting aspects of this particular brave new world. Maybe the rising tide of digital novelty will eventually retreat, driven back by a shaming awareness of the terrible predicament new technology has created. Yes, we can instantaneously send anyone anywhere on earth our latest video of a surfboarding hamster.

But at what price? Research has been undermined; newspapers, magazines and books have been devalued or destroyed. Cinema will soon be ruined. Sex has become trashy commerce. Momentary celebrity bests enduring fame. Truth has been relativised, while airborne robots will monitor our every activity and smartphones betray us hourly. Uber knows more about us than our parents did. A more connected world may well be an uglier, more brutish one.

Of course, brands have not disappeared. It is just that past favourites have been replaced by Google, Uber and Facebook, or whatever is coming next. With the prospect of ever more intrusive surveillance endangering our personal liberty, and with the threat of sin-sector branding being outlawed, it is easy to look back at the old brand culture and wonder at the charming innocence of it all. What a fine world it was when all you needed to experience deliciousness and refreshment was a five cent Coke. When drinking Irish stout was good for you. When possession of a German car gave access to the ultimate modernist experience of engaging to the full in mechanical technology. When a woman smoking a cigarette was, in fact, carrying a torch of freedom. When toilet tissue was a luxury and a Martini turned you into a handsome cosmopolitan lothario.

That all seems so wistful now. In this reading, brands are certainly history. But history may have a future.

'What a fine world it was when all you needed to experience deliciousness and refreshment was a five cent Coke'

APPENDIX

The 10 principles of great brands.

1. Like any successful design, great branding should be timeless and consistent, but, at the same time, capable of development. You refresh, but you do not replace.

2. 'Brand' has become a metonym for 'product'. But it is also more than the product, including all the meanings surrounding it. A great brand is at the centre of a whole culture.

3. Data from wind tunnels tends to force similarity on the shape of modern cars. In marketing, everyone has access to the same consumer metrics. John Hegarty calls this "wind tunnel marketing". Great brands are all the same... in that they are different to the norm.

4. Great brands do not lie. They tell attractive truths about quality, consistency and pleasure.

5. Great brands are never boring.

6. And you can never simply invent a great brand. It's a collaboration between many disciplines over time. An excellent product is a necessary, but not sufficient, starting point.

7. Great brands are immediately recognisable, even when their precise identity is obscured.

8. Great brands tell stories.

9. People like them.

10. Because of this, really great brands never die.

BIBLIOGRAPHY

Isadore Barmash, Always Live Better Than Your Clients, Dodd Mead, 1984

Stephen Bayley, Harley Earl and the Dream Machine, Weidenfeld, 1983

Stephen Bayley, Coke! designing a megabrand, Boilerhouse Project, 1986

Stephen Bayley, The Lucky Strike Packet by Raymond Loewy, Verlag Form, 1998

Daniel Boorstin, The Image – a guide to pseudo-events in America, Vintage, 1962

Gordon Bruce, Eliot Noyes, Phaidon, 2006

Claire Fox, I Find That Offensive, Biteback, 2016

John Hegarty, Hegarty on Advertising, Thames and Hudson, 2011

Naomi Klein, No Logo, Knopf, 1999

Raymond Loewy, Never Leave Well Enough Alone, Simon & Schuster, 1951

George Lois, The Art of Advertising, H.N. Abrams, 1977

Alfredo Marcantonio, Remember Those Great Volkswagen Ads?, Merrell, 2014

Stanley Moss, What is a Brand?, HcT Press, 2016

David Ogilvy, On Advertising, Macmillan, 1983

Wally Olins, The Corporate Personality, Design Council, 1979

Wally Olins, On Brand, Thames and Hudson, 2003

Jonathan Price, The Best Things on TV, Penguin, 1979

Rosser Reeves, Reality in Advertising, Knopf, 1961

Elaine Scarry, On Beauty and Being Just, Princeton University Press, 1999

Luc Sante, No Smoking, Assouline, 2004

Thorstein Veblen, The Theory of the Leisure Class, Macmillan, 1899

Andy Warhol, The Philosophy of Andy Warhol, Harcourt Brace Jovanovich, 1975

Tom Wolfe, Chester Gould Versus Roy Lichtenstein, Los Angeles County Museum of Art, 1976

ABOUT THIS BOOK

In 1979 London's Design Council, then the nation's most influential voice in these matters, published two books. One was Wally Olins' Corporate Personality, the other was my own In Good Shape. Mine was about product design, Olins' was about branding. Straws in the wind, perhaps.

Each was among the first in its field. I admired Olins' unsentimental, even hard-nosed, approach to his subject, but was very suspicious about the notion of 'branding'. I always felt, and still do, that, in business, solid product has priority over vapid fluff.

But as our world has become progressively post-industrial and globalised – two converging vectors that will surely converge in misery – I have begun to modify my views. While still sceptical about the true value of telling a butch building contractor to put cute humming birds on his high-pressure compressors to enhance his 'brand' (a job that made Olins' fortune), it's now a real world fact that businesses are valued at least as much for their associated metaphors and meanings as they are for their hardware or material assets.

And since symbolism and iconography fascinate, I have become ever more interested in what's actually meant by brand. The Andrex Puppy cannot, perhaps, be compared to Michelangelo's Moses in terms of aesthetic value, but the role it plays in the acceptance of a manufacturer of two-ply toilet tissue is directly comparable to the role the Pope Julius II tomb played in the acceptance of the della Rovere family and the Roman Catholic Church. That's not blasphemy, it's observed fact.

Since we have, alas, lost access to religious parables and mythological tales, brands supply many of the meaningful narratives in everyday life. For good or for bad, commercial culture is now the majority source of our ideas about style, taste, fashion and desire. Possibly even morals, but probably less so. Talking of the patronage of artists, the great designer George Nelson once said: "You either have the Church or you have IBM." IBM has now gone the way the Roman Empire... but only to be replaced by Apple or Samsung or whoever is the current or next market darling.

So because there are pleasure and instruction to be found in the observation of brands, because they demand public engagement with (and potential criticism of) commerce and industry, the emerging international movement to outlaw branding of cigarettes and impose in its place anhedonic generic packaging deliberately designed to deter and dismay is deplorable. It's a curious moment in consumer culture when designers are legally required to produce something that's deliberately ugly. There are disturbing grounds to believe that if packaging of cigarettes be banned, so too can the packaging and promotion of other products of debatable value. I'm against it, so JTI (Japan Tobacco International) supported the printing of this little polemical book. Of course, opinions expressed here are my own and not JTI's.

To be sure, I am not a smoker. I actually dislike smoking very much and have no enthusiasm for promoting tobacco interests. But I dislike even more the mentality that wants to inhibit free consumer choice of products that are not illegal. I don't endorse alcohol-fuelled wife-beating, suicidal ingestion of refined sugar and the carnage of road traffic accidents, but nor do I want to suppress the branding and promotion of beer, chocolate biscuits and cars. Better educated behaviour is the answer to social and health problems arising out of our various appetites, not the slitty-eyed and thin-lipped banning mentality.

INDEX

PICTURE CREDITS

Acknowledgements:
With thanks to : Vanessa Bird for the index,
Nick Coomber for the artwork, Ilana Harris for the
proof reading, Lizzie Mercer for the design,
Caroline Penn for the picture research
and Ted Ryan for his Coke bottle.